AF255657

"Everyone who reads *The Seven Storey Mountain* wants to know more about Thomas Merton's only brother, John Paul. William J. Meegan's *Remembering the Forgotten Merton* pieces together meticulously researched historical fragments to truly bring John Paul Merton to life. He is no longer forgotten."

—**Paul M. Pearson**
Director and archivist, Thomas Merton Center

"This well-researched and engaging book provides readers with an extraordinary glimpse into the short life of John Paul Merton, the younger brother of the renowned spiritual writer and Trappist monk Thomas Merton. Not only does William J. Meegan shine a light on the 'forgotten Merton,' giving the younger brother his own due, but this book also provides new insight and context for understanding the childhood and early adult years of his famous older brother. I highly recommend this book."

—**Daniel P. Horan, OFM**
Professor of philosophy, Saint Mary's College, Notre Dame

"William J. Meegan invites us to remember John Paul as he was—not just the monk-writer's younger brother but a brave and deeply spiritual person in his own right. Thus, John Paul's life—with all its twists and turns, its troubles and triumphs—becomes a reminder that God is to be sought and found in the ordinary. Meticulously researched and written with clarity and grace, this book contributes significantly to our understanding of the whole Merton family. It is a must-read!"

—**Christine M. Bochen**
Professor emerita of religious studies, Nazareth College

Remembering
the Forgotten Merton

Remembering
the Forgotten Merton

WILLIAM J. MEEGAN

With Foreword by
Christopher Pramuk

WIPF & STOCK · Eugene, Oregon

Wipf & Stock
An Imprint of Wipf and Stock Publishers
199 W. 8th Ave., Suite 3
Eugene, OR 97401

www.wipfandstock.com

PAPERBACK ISBN: 978-1-6667-3053-1
HARDCOVER ISBN: 978-1-6667-2218-5
EBOOK ISBN: 978-1-6667-2219-2

VERSION NUMBER 012723

Contents

Tables

Foreword

God has a very fresh and living memory of the smallest and most forgotten.

—Bartolomé de las Casas

While reading William Meegan's poignant and meticulously researched account of John Paul Merton, the forgotten one, I couldn't help thinking of the American Jesuit priest and theologian Fr. William F. Lynch. Like Bill Meegan, Bill Lynch was especially interested in what he called the "smaller line" of history, those hidden and less celebrated persons and events, as Meegan puts it, "to which others have not given much attention." Like Bill Meegan—and much in the spirit of Thomas Merton—Bill Lynch believed that it is only by embracing the limitations, the poverty, the smallness of actual human lives that we come to realize the greater and larger part, the likeness of God, the law of love, written into our very being. For Lynch, the breathtaking irony of a mature Christian faith is that we are given to see the revelation of God in the apparent "weakness" of human life: the Messiah who was born in a stable; the king who entered Jerusalem on a donkey; the teacher who embraced lepers, ate with sinners, and proclaimed freedom for prisoners; the executed one who was raised and exalted as Lord.

If John Paul Merton's story has largely disappeared beneath the legacy of his famous elder brother, Bill Meegan invites us to look again, and more deeply. Like most of us whose names will never be recorded in the "larger line" of history, John Paul's "is a story of a quietly lived spirituality." *A life that began singing in a crib was to end praying in a dinghy.* After reading Bill's beautiful book, I couldn't agree more with his stated purpose. By looking back at John Paul's life, "we may just find the inspiration to look forward in a loving way, as he did."

To borrow Bill's proverbial image of his decades-long search for John Paul, we are all needles in the haystack, hidden eternally, as his elder brother reassured us, yet never for a moment forgotten, in the ever-greater mystery of God. With this book Bill has not only gifted us with "a fresh approach to the brothers Merton." In illuminating the life of the forgotten one, he invites each of us to notice, and honor, the hidden contours of our own.

A last thought that I can't escape. Thomas Merton came into the world on "the last day of January 1915, under the sign of the Water Bearer, in a year of a great war." John Paul passed out of this world in April of 1943, under the shadow of another great war, which ended in a spasm of genocidal and nuclear holocaust. His final act, as Bill notes, was an act of courage and love for others, calling forth "a degree of selflessness rarely found without a deep spirituality." As I write these lines, rumors of the Unspeakable, a third global war, are beginning to howl. Russian tanks and aircraft are attacking the Ukrainian people in a hail fire of missiles and cluster bombs, destroying infrastructure and murdering without discrimination. A new generation beholds with horror the machinery of war, its power to turn life into senseless death with the pull of a trigger. And while the mad architect evokes the nuclear threat on all who would stand against him, the world stands in mute wonder at the courage and resistance of the Ukrainian people. How many more final acts of courage, of resistance, of selfless love for others will it take to convince the human race that we are destined for so much more than the banal evil and cruelty of war?

Where, in what desolate and smoky country, / Lies your poor body, lost and dead?

And in what landscape of disaster / Has your unhappy spirit lost its road?

The elder brother's poem of regret and love for his younger brother—Tom's unforgettable coda to *The Seven Storey Mountain*—has never spoken more powerfully to me than it does today. May John Paul's journey of hidden holiness beckon to us as a prayer of hope for all humanity, that we may never cease striving to become who we are, brothers and sisters of God, and learn to know, with renewed compassion, "the Christ of the burnt men."

Christopher Pramuk, PhD
Regis University Chair of
Ignatian Thought and Imagination

Preface

The life and writings of Thomas Merton have been a predominant interest of mine for many years. The Merton Study Group at the Abbey of Gethsemani, near Bardstown, Kentucky, facilitated by Br. Paul Quenon, OCSO, was a part of my regular monthly schedule. So, when Dr. Bill Paulsell, a local Merton scholar, gave me a copy of James Forest's *Thomas Merton: A Pictorial Biography*, I was set to enjoy a good read. But I was surprised to find that the person of his brother, John Paul, leapt off the pages. I re-read some of Thomas Merton's works in a new light.

References to John Paul are few and brief in Merton's autobiography, *The Seven Storey Mountain*, and in all of Thomas Merton's other works. Trying to learn about John Paul through his brother was like hunting for the proverbial needle in a haystack. The sequel to the autobiography, *The Sign of Jonas*, includes only one reference to John Paul. Michael Mott, Thomas Merton's official biographer, has little information about John Paul in *The Seven Mountains of Thomas Merton*.

As I commented on this newfound interest to others who were familiar with Thomas Merton, something became apparent: some who knew Thomas Merton's writing well said they didn't know he had a brother. Others knew of Merton's brother but could not remember his name. Those who knew his name knew very little about his life. It became clear that John Paul was the forgotten Merton.

Who was John Paul, beyond the fact that he was Thomas Merton's brother? How did his life unfold? How did he handle the loss of his parents? What was his relationship to his brother Thomas like? These are some of the questions that led me to pursue research about John Paul's life. This narrative is based on details about him from his brother Tom's writings as well as other texts by notable authors and newly discovered records. My research included data from census, church, school, and military records, letters from and about John Paul, as well as ship passenger lists, federal draft records, and multiple national and international websites devoted to World War II data and records. Each record brought John Paul into greater focus.

Certainly, our undertakings have many motives, some of which we are aware and others more elusive. The motives that prompted my search for John Paul Merton's story are varied. As I re-read biographies of Thomas Merton with an eye to details about John Paul, I developed a kinship with him. Maybe my pursuit of John Paul's life story is because I am also a younger brother who looked up to an older brother and tagged along with him at the behest of our mother. He was certainly not willing to include me. My brother was six years older than I and hung out with a bunch of rough-necks in our Brooklyn neighborhood. While they did not throw stones at me, as Tom did to John Paul, they did manage to climb ten-foot-high fences topped with barbed wire, in their efforts to get rid of me. They thought I could not or would not follow them. If I was to stay with my brother, I had to climb the fence or be left behind. I climbed the fence. My brother was a tough kid and I wanted to be just as tough and athletic. I wore his old boots which were too large for me, shagged balls for his softball team, and treasured the secondhand team jacket he gave me.

This is somewhat the same position John Paul was in during his early childhood. Admittedly the times are different by about twenty-five years, and certainly, Douglaston, Queens, in the 1920s was not the Bushwick section of Brooklyn in the 1950s. But the circumstances of the two fraternal relationships were similar: Tom did not want John Paul around anymore than my brother wanted me, and John Paul struggled to keep up with Tom, as I did with my brother. John Paul persisted in his attempts to stay attached to his brother despite barriers, although there were no ten-foot-high chain-link fences in his story.

Another possible motive for my pursuit of John Paul's story could stem from my interest in topics to which others have not given much attention. In my training as a clinical psychologist, there was little attention paid to patients considered resistant to therapy. They were labeled as untreatable. I was interested in learning how to care for these patients. Later in my career, at the time I began my study of the psychology of forgiveness in the late 1980s, the topic was relegated to theology or literature and not to be discussed in psychological circles. Yet my interest led me to develop courses in the psychology of forgiveness that I taught for many years.

My education as a clinical psychologist included training with the founders of family therapy (Haley, Whitaker, Minuchin) and led to my clinical practice of more than forty years working with families in distress. As I worked with families, it became clear that what held them together was the ability to accept each other as they were and to forgive each other for their limitations. Eventually I taught courses in family therapy and forgiveness and reconciliation in the graduate programs of the Psychology Department of the University of Kentucky and at the Lexington Theological Seminary in Lexington, Kentucky.

The relationship of the Merton brothers, as well as their three-generational family system, was immediately of interest to me. Some of the questions that caught my attention and that I explore in this book are: How did a sibling rivalry, expressed only by the older brother, develop between the brothers? How did the older brother, an intellectual, relate to a younger brother who was an impulsive person of action? How did grandparents continue to support their grandchildren despite their dislike of the children's father (a single parent)? I was intrigued by John Paul, who managed to avoid the possible negative outcomes of the early loss of his mother, rejection by his father, being ignored by his brother, and the many other disappointments of his life.

In some part, also, my interest was due to a sense of awe at John Paul's heroism during World War II. He remains a model of selflessness and deep spirituality.

Having considered the question of why I might be interested in John Paul Merton, the more significant question is why anyone else would be interested in his story. His story illustrates a quietly lived spirituality, that there is not one mold for living a holy life. John Paul's path was ordinary until his heroic end. Each of us can identify with having unrealized challenges and hopes and failed aspirations. But more significantly, most of us can recognize in our own experience John Paul's ordinary, seemingly insignificant spiritual journey from his grade school days at the Cathedral school to the door of the Abbey at Gethsemani, where his spiritual transformation kicked into high gear. There is a little bit of him in each of us. By looking back at his life, we may find the inspiration to look forward in a loving way, as he did.

My research uncovered new dimensions of the Merton family that were previously unknown. The story of the interpersonal relationships shed light on the dynamics of the nuclear Merton family and contribute to more nuanced future research. Viewing John Paul's relationship with his brother through the lens of historical fact casts a new perspective on Thomas. We see the features of John Paul and Tom's characters and the life events that they had to overcome as they grew into adulthood. Impulsiveness shaped John Paul's early life; self-centeredness shaped Tom's. For both boys, the loss of parents at an early age was a crisis that affected their development. The more we know about the Merton family, the more we can see our shared humanity.

John Paul is the focus and his brother Tom the background for this book. As the research progressed, the temptation to be distracted by the events of Tom's life was difficult to resist. In *The Seven Storey Mountain*, the events are written from Tom's point of view, which is natural since he was writing his own biography. The challenge of describing John Paul's experience was that little firsthand or personal documentation either by him or about him exists. I could not write the book from John Paul's point of view. Thus, I simply followed the facts, and having done so, brought my clinical experience to bear on interpretation of the normal psychological response to the events John Paul experienced. His life was marked by the repeated tragedy of losing parents, one after the other, and then losing the loving parental figures who raised him (his grandparents). Somehow, he remained optimistic, loving, open-hearted, and deeply spiritual.

The brother of John Paul described in this story is not the famous monk and author many know. The person of Tom was not the person of Father Louis Merton, OCSO. Rather, Tom in this narrative is first a child and then a young man who is not yet famous. He is simply a son and brother in a family. He is an aspiring writer and yet to be a famous monk. He is referred to as "Tom" throughout this story. This is also in keeping with the way his mother preferred to call him.

My intent for this biography is to adhere to the recommendation made by Ed Rice and focus on details that can be documented. Rice regretted various inaccurate facts about Thomas Merton being passed on from one author to another without efforts to document the sources. This point of view applies to the entire Merton family, and I have tried to explore the truth of the various events of this family as far as witnesses and documentation allowed.

Acknowledgments

THEY SAY IT TAKES a village to raise a child. It took a village of mentors to bring this book into being. The support and encouragement of Sheila Milton gave me the impetus to begin the research and writing of this story. The earliest versions were read by William Paulsell, PhD, Former Dean of the Lexington Theological Seminary, Christopher Pramuk, PhD, Regis University Chair of Ignatian Thought and Imagination, and John Gorman, a personal friend. Their encouragement allowed me to pursue the project.

Margaret Nutting Ralph, PhD, a published author of many texts, and Paul Pearson, PhD, Director of the Thomas Merton Center at Bellarmine University, read drafts and offered comments.

I owe a debt of gratitude to John James Merton, first cousin of Thomas and John Paul Merton, and to Roger Collins, art historian, both of New Zealand, who shared knowledge of Merton family stories. My thanks to the monks of the Abbey of Gethsemani for their help, support, and guidance.

My thanks go out to all the people at libraries, churches, universities, and museums who patiently answered questions and pointed me in the right direction to the resources I sought, and also to Albert Romkema of Petawawa, Canada, for sharing artifacts with me. I am in debt to my friend and editor, Mary Donnelly, without whom this book would not have been completed.

Thanks to my children and their spouses for listening, commenting, and reassuring me and for their continual help managing word processing dead ends and organizing files.

My wife, Kathleen, whose support was ever present, deserves the ultimate recognition for her constant smile.

1

The Genesis of John Paul Merton[1]

Introduction

UNRAVELING THE LIFE OF the forgotten son and brother in the Merton family ought to begin at the beginning, which raises the question: Where is the beginning? Does it start in the Flushing neighborhood of New York City where John Paul Merton was born? That would mean interpreting the word *beginning* to mean the geography of his beginning. If so, why not begin in the village of Redgrave, Suffolk, England, where Anthony Murton, one of the earliest known members of the Merton family, was born in 1652?[2] Anthony Murton was a poor farmer who worked the land owned by others. The geographic beginning could also be Scotland, where his paternal grandmother, Gertrude Grierson, traced her roots to Sir Gilbert Grierson in 1353, the First Lord of Lag, Dumfriesshire, Scotland.[3] The Griersons were landed gentry and lords of the realm. The distant ancestry of his maternal grandmother, Martha Baldwin, might be the starting point for

1. This chapter relies heavily on Roger Collins's unpublished manuscript titled "Sense of Construction: The Life and Work of Owen Merton," provided by The Merton Center at Bellarmine University. Because the pagination of each chapter begins with page 1, the citations of this work note both the chapter number followed by the page number: Collins, "Sense of Construction," chapter X, Y.

2. Meegan, "Paternal Ancestors of Thomas Merton," 16.

3. "Clan Grierson History."

1

John Paul's story. Martha Baldwin's roots can be traced to Jesse Baldwin, of the Quaker community of Deep River, Guilford, North Carolina (1779),[4] a farmer who later moved to Ohio. We could look, instead, to Cardiganshire, Wales, where his third great grandfather on the maternal side, Arthur Jenkins, was married in 1787.[5] Arthur Jenkins had fled religious persecution at the turn of the century and was in search of arable farmland, which he found in Bristol Township, Morgan County, Ohio.[6]

These beginnings of John Paul's remote heritage may be historically informative; however, such exploration could draw our attention away from the person himself: John Paul Merton. Exploring the lives of his parents is not too remote, either in geography or chronology, from the place and time in which he came to be.

A new beginning suggests a new creation. John Paul was created (i.e., brought into existence) through the love of his parents, Owen Heathcote Grierson Merton and Ruth Calvert Jenkins, who, as art students in France, met and fell in love at a time and in a place overflowing with aspiring artists from all over the world. The energy of their mutual attraction is the beginning, the spark that ignited their love and from which came their sons Thomas and John Paul. The beginning of Ruth and Owen's relationship is the true beginning of the life of John Paul.

To assist the reader, the table below presents the family and friends of John Paul Merton, their names and their relationship to John Paul.

Table 1—Family and Friends of John Paul Merton

Last Name, First Name	Relationship to John Paul Merton
Cleary, Father	Catholic Chaplain, Cornell University
Evans, John Albert Kay	Father-in-law
Evans, Margaret May	Wife
Griffin, Reverend William	Catholic priest, performed marriage ceremony for Margaret and John Paul
Hadingham, Eric G.	RCAF Squadron 166 rear gunner, survived crash
Hart, Robert	RCAF Squadron 166 roommate and friend, named son for John Paul
Hauck, Walter	Brother of Elsie Hauck Holahan Jenkins, wrote to John Paul during WWII

4. U.S. Quaker Meeting Records (1681–1935).

5. Cardiganshire, Wales, Anglican Baptisms, Marriages, and Burials (1633–1993).

6. Meegan, "Maternal Ancestors of Thomas Merton."

Last Name, First Name	Relationship to John Paul Merton
Holahan, Patricia	Daughter of Elsie Hauck Holahan Jenkins, teenage friend of John Paul
Holahan, Patrick	First husband of Elsie Hauck Holahan Jenkins
Jenkins, Elsie Hauck Holahan	Wife of Harold Jenkins (second husband), caretaker of Mattie Jenkins and possibly John Paul as infant
Jenkins, Harold	Maternal uncle
Jenkins, Martha (Mattie) Baldwin	Maternal grandmother
Jenkins, Samuel	Maternal grandfather
Lord, Roderick Alan	RCAF Squadron 166 navigator, survived crash
Lupton, Sidney Jacques	RCAF Squadron 166 pilot, died in crash
Merton, Alfred James	Paternal grandfather
Merton, Gertrude Grierson	Paternal grandmother
Merton, Owen Heathcote	Father
Merton, Ruth Jenkins	Mother
Merton, Thomas	Brother
Miscall, Len	Friend in Ithaca
Miscall, Rovene	Friend in Ithaca, wife of Len, executrix of John Paul's will
Pearce, Ben	Husband of Emily Maud Pearce
Pearce, Emily Maud Grierson	The sister of Owen Merton's mother
Riley, Reverend Lester	Episcopal priest, baptized John Paul 1929
Trier, Erwin	Husband of Aunt Gwynedd Merton Trier
Trier, Gwynedd Merton	Paternal aunt
Whitfield, William Forster	RCAF Squadron 166 wireless operator, died in crash

Ruth Jenkins and Owen Merton

Ruth

Ruth Jenkins was born on June 12, 1887,[7] in Zanesville, Ohio, to Martha Caroline Jenkins (nee Baldwin) (1862–1937)[8] and Samuel Adams Jenkins

7. Ohio, Births and Christenings Index (1774–1973).
8. "Ruth Calvert Jenkins Merton."

(1862–1936).[9] Martha, known as Mattie, was the youngest of four girls. Her father, Daniel Baldwin, was a machinist. Little is known of Mattie's mother, Maria. Before marriage, Mattie worked as a bookkeeper for her sister Lizzie's husband, Samuel Ebert, who owned a Fancy Goods shop.[10]

Sam Jenkins was the youngest of five boys[11] born to James Jenkins (1831–1876) and Mary Adams Jenkins (1830–1879). James left farming to become a peddler, selling dry goods and sundries carried on an open wagon pulled by a horse through the street. James died when Sam was fourteen years old; his mother, Mary, died when he was sixteen years old. As a sixteen-year-old orphan, he struck out on his own and worked as a newsboy, finally managing to purchase a stationery store. In 1885, at age twenty-three, he married Mattie C. Baldwin.[12] His store on Main Street in Zanesville, Ohio—Jenkins Bazaar—sold newspapers, magazines, books, stationery, rubber stamps, and other goods. The Zanesville Opera House was on the same street. Sam specialized in opera librettos. He had a reputation for whistling many of the arias in the store in a rather bombastic way. It is likely that Mattie's bookkeeping skills helped to grow Sam's business into a book, stationery, and art store.[13] Sam eventually sold the store in 1898 to T. H. Edmiston.[14] After selling his store, Sam's business life had several twists and turns.

As a regular book salesman to Sam's Bazaar, George Dunlap admired Sam's retail methods. Around the time Sam sold his stationery store, Dunlap was forming a partnership with Alexander Grosset to start a publishing firm; he offered Sam a partnership in the new company. Sam turned down the offer, taking a job with the American Tract Society in Philadelphia.[15] He then worked briefly as a salesman for Grosset and Dunlap Publishers and later moved to Cleveland, Ohio, to work for the Burrows Brothers publishing firm. His dream had been to work on the East Coast; he eventually (around 1900) worked his way east to New York City, where he was again offered a position at Grosset and Dunlap publishing house in New

<hr>

9. Ohio, Births and Christenings Index (1774–1973).

10. U.S. Federal Census (1880), Zanesville, OH, 375B.

11. U.S. Federal Census (1870), Zanesville, OH, 526B.

12. Ohio, Births and Christenings Index (1774–1973).

13. U.S. City Directories (1822–1995).

14. "Obituary: Samuel Jenkins."

15. At the time, the American Tract Society was a nonprofit, nonsectarian organization devoted to spreading Christian literature.

York City. At first, Sam was a traveling salesman in New England. He had a way of showing booksellers how to sell more books through a marketing scheme. These schemes were his strong suit, and when publishing novelized versions of successful plays became popular, his talent for promotion and merchandising became well-known in the publishing business. He brought the same talent to selling books about popular movies, a tactic that made Grosset and Dunlap very successful. He became marketing director for the publishing company, a promotion that made him a wealthy man. His was a career success story: from a newsboy selling newspapers on street corners to a white-collar executive.[16]

Sometime around 1914, Sam moved his family from Manhattan to Douglaston, in the borough of Queens, New York City, into a family home that had been designed and built by his son Harold, Ruth's elder brother, who was an engineer.[17] The family's lifestyle included household staff: a maid, a cook, a cleaning lady, and a personal companion for his wife Mattie, who suffered from diabetes.

Ruth attended elementary school at St. Agatha School and high school at the Wadleigh School (both in Manhattan). Wadleigh (now the Wadleigh High School for the Performing and Visual Arts), still on West 114th Street, was the first public high school for girls in New York City.[18] The Wadleigh mission then, as now, was to coach and develop young women "to pursue their dreams and passions in order to become productive members of society."[19]

Following graduation from Wadleigh, Ruth completed a three-year course in general studies at Bradford Academy in Haverhill, Massachusetts.[20] The curriculum focused primarily on the arts, dance, and writing, as well as the humanities. In order to be accepted each student was required to present a certificate of good moral character from the principal of her previous school and one from the pastor of her church. Ruth's academic record was of the level that she was admitted without examination. Ruth had a graceful spirit, an ingenious imagination, and an honest sense of humor (she was known to entertain her classmates each evening by dancing

---

16. "Obituary: Samuel Jenkins."
17. Collins, "Sense of Construction," chapter 12, 1.
18. "Wadleigh High School for Girls."
19. "Mission and Vision."
20. *The Bradford Annual Catalog (1908–1909)*, 42.

in the parlor of the residence hall).[21] She was named the cleverest and most artistic student in her graduating class of 1909.

In May 1910, both Ruth and her mother applied for passports in anticipation of a trip to Europe; Ruth stated she planned to stay for two years, while Mattie planned to stay for eight months.[22] The itinerary details remain unknown. Ruth travelled with her mother and arrived in London on June 20, 1910.[23] Harold left New York City in July[24] and returned with his mother in October 1910.[25] Passenger list records for Sam's travel were not able to be found. Ruth remained in Paris, enrolling in the Écoles des Arts Décoratifs to study interior decorating. She took painting classes from Percyval Tudor-Hart afterward, where she met Owen Merton.

Owen

Owen Merton was born on May 14, 1887 to Alfred James Merton and Gertrude Hannah Merton (nee Grierson) in Christchurch, New Zealand.[26] His grandfather Charles Merton (1821–1885) was one of the earliest English settlers to arrive in New Zealand from Suffolk, England, in 1856. The family had deep ties to the Anglican faith: Owen's father was a musician and singer who taught at Christ's College, an Anglican boys' school modeled on the English public school system. Alfred Merton was school organist and choirmaster from 1878 through 1918; he founded a band and an orchestra, composed the school song, and served at the heart of the school's corporate life. He was also organist at the Anglican Cathedral of Christchurch.[27]

Owen's mother, Gertrude, was born in Cardiff, Wales, in 1855, and her family immigrated to New Zealand in 1864. Gertrude suffered from poliomyelitis from childhood.[28] Collins notes:

> Doubtless because of this early handicap she was at first educated at home but later attended classes at the Collegiate Union, walking from Avonside to attend evening lectures. She passed the

21. Collins, "Sense of Construction," chapter 8, 11.

22. U.S. Passport Applications (1795–1925).

23. U.K. Incoming Passenger Lists (1910), piece 439.

24. U.K. Incoming Passenger Lists (1910), piece 598.

25. New York, Passenger Lists (1910).

26. New Zealand, Birth Index (1840–1950).

27. Collins, "Sense of Construction," chapter 1, 8.

28. Collins, "Sense of Construction," chapter 1, 6.

Matriculation Examination at Canterbury College in 1877, and studied there, but did not graduate for she had no mathematics, at that time a compulsory subject for a degree.[29]

Gertrude was educated and anxious to pursue her own career. She became a schoolteacher, then opened her own school, and later, taught in a private school for a time and taught private pupils as well.[30]

Owen's artistic talent was recognized by age eight, when he started school at Christ's College in 1895. He received prizes in music and drawing, and he sang in the chapel choir.[31] In the spring term of 1903 (at age sixteen), he enrolled in the School of Art associated with Canterbury College. In 1904 (at age seventeen), at his Aunt Maud's invitation and her expense, he left New Zealand to study art in London.[32] His Aunt Maud (Emily Maud Mary Grierson), his mother's sister, had both the means and the inclination to support his artistic endeavors, something his parents could not afford. The youngest of Gertrude's siblings, Maud was married to Ben Pearce,[33] who had been headmaster of Durston House Preparatory School for Boys;[34] they lived in West London. The couple was a continuous source of support for Owen in the years to come. Aunt Maud was Owen's first patron.

Owen spent the next three years studying art, returning to Christchurch in 1907 (at age twenty), where he continued to work on his painting and hold exhibitions. Over the next two years, he had some success: by late 1909, he had returned to London, where he studied under Charles van Havermaet until he went to Paris in the autumn of 1910. In Paris, he studied at Colarossi's studio for a year, and in the summer of 1911 (at age twenty-four), he began studies with the Canadian artist, Percyval Tudor-Hart.[35]

Thus it was that John Paul Merton's parents-to-be both came from families consisting of strong people who were self-starters, people who valued and practiced the arts, and who believed in the abilities and potential of their children. That Ruth Jenkins was both schooled beyond high school and encouraged to pursue her interests abroad at a time when women were still considered property in many households and that Owen Merton

29. Collins, "Sense of Construction," chapter 1, 6.

30. Collins, "Sense of Construction," chapter 1, 6.

31. Collins, "Sense of Construction," chapter 1, 19.

32. Collins, "Sense of Construction," chapter 1, 17.

33. London, England, Church of England Marriages (1754–1932).

34. England Census Class RG14.

35. Collins, "Sense of Construction," chapter 8, 2.

was enabled, by parents of modest means, to travel from New Zealand to England to study painting while still a teenager is truly extraordinary. The chance that these two people, so unusual in the context of the history of their time, should meet in a place far removed from their homes of origin, seems so remote as to be implausible. Yet this is just one extraordinary event that brought to life a man who, though outwardly appeared unaccomplished, carried within himself an interior journey that would reveal itself only in the shining, astonishing moment of his death.

1911 to 1916: Courtship and Marriage

In Paris, Ruth studied first at the Écoles des Arts Décoratifs. Sometime in the summer of 1911, Ruth met Percyval Tudor-Hart and enrolled in his studio. He offered a sketching/painting class in the summer of 1911, in the Pyrenees Mountains in the southwestern corner of France on the border with Spain (Catalonia), where the scenery and light were unique. Students gathered in the countryside, harbor, village, or wherever their mentor was teaching, but each found his or her own place to live. Whether Owen and Ruth had previously met is not clear but both enrolled in Tudor-Hart's class.[36]

Fonterrabia is a village on the Spanish side of the Bidassoa Bay; across the bay is the French village of Hendaye. Owen stayed in Fonterrabia, and Ruth stayed across the bay in Hendaye. Later that year, Owen wrote to his mother that he "went across the bay to call on an American girl."[37] His use of the phrase "call on" suggests this trip across the bay was more than just catching up with the others from Tudor-Hart's studio. He was searching out Ruth, with whom he had been smitten. And so, during a summer art class in July 1911, their relationship began.

During this class, Owen, Ruth, and Tudor-Hart worked together, each sketching the Chateau at Fonterrabia; Owen would have spent time with Ruth alone while sketching.

Following the end of Tudor-Hart's class, in the autumn of 1911, Ruth returned to Paris and sublet Owen's Parisian flat while Owen stayed in the Pyrenees to paint. On his return to Paris, Owen was astounded by the way she had cleaned and decorated the rooms.

36. Collins, "Sense of Construction," chapter 8, 8.
37. Collins, "Sense of Construction," chapter 8, 10.

What are the odds of these two people from opposite sides of the globe meeting and falling in love? How likely is it that a well-bred young lady from New York City would meet an aspiring artist from Christchurch, New Zealand? Their relationship blossomed in Paris, where the Seine River sparkles, the French language is romantic, Parisienne fashion is ahead of its time, and the skyline is magnificent.

In December, Owen described Ruth to his mother in a letter:

> The American girl who had my Studio in October is one of those good sorts, who can really be friends, and she has a head full of interesting things, though she don't [sic] know much about painting.[38]

Owen was so infatuated with Ruth that, even before asking her to marry him, he told his mother they were engaged.[39]

Ruth rejected Owen's proposal of marriage, made some time in the winter months of 1911–1912. She was not planning on a marriage at the time. Living in the country of her dreams and enjoying life with other art students, she reveled in the culture and language of France. She lived with a friend, Grace Roosevelt,[40] in a flat at 29 Rue Madame in the sixth arrondissement, within walking distance of the Luxembourg Gardens and the Boulevard Montparnasse. While she had no interest in an engagement, Ruth did not spurn Owen's attention. Owen spent as much time with her as he could and persuaded her to accept a five-year plan: they would marry in five years if both remained uncommitted to others.

Owen was persistent, persuasive, and unabashedly in love. By August 1912, the five-year moratorium was terminated, and Ruth accepted his proposal.[41] In October 1912, Owen moved to 59 Rue Bonaparte, purportedly to save money and to be nearer to Tudor-Hart's studio, but incidentally, it was much closer to Ruth's flat. They shared meals, outings, and a wide range of friends from America and Europe. They took trips to Chantilly, Fontainebleau, and eventually, to the Provence region of France. They also traveled to Italy.

38. Collins, "Sense of Construction," chapter 8, 9.
39. Collins, "Sense of Construction," chapter 8, 13.
40. Collins, "Sense of Construction," chapter 9, 4
41. Collins, "Sense of Construction," chapter 8, 12.

Ruth and Owen in France, circa 1912. Used with permission of the Merton Legacy Trust and the Thomas Merton Center at Bellarmine University.

Both were conscious of how much money they would need to marry, since neither expected to be rich, but neither did they want to risk living the typical life of a starving artist. Ruth had been raised in an upper middle-class family and knew little deprivation. Her tuition at Bradford Academy of $600/year in the early 1900s was equivalent to approximately $17,000 today.[42]

Owen's family, while not poor, had limited resources and could not afford his education in Paris, which was funded by his Aunt Maud. Neither Owen nor Ruth thought about finances in global terms; it is not likely they had any notion of the specifics of a family budget. Owen thought it would take £300 in annual salary (equivalent to approximately £35,000 in 2021) and £200 in savings (approximately £23,400 in 2021)[43] for them to marry.[44] He set about painting more, and his parents in New Zealand acted as his agents to set up shows of his paintings there.

Ruth studied painting not in order to paint but to sharpen her skills for interior decorating. On December 20, 1911, she wrote to Tudor-Hart:

42. "CPI Inflation Calculator."

43. "Inflation Calculator."

44. Collins, "Sense of Construction," chapter 8, 23.

> The sort of work I am preparing to do—which is to influence
> people by creating an appropriate environment for them: there
> is no more fascinating subject in the world than the influence of
> surroundings on human character. And to study character with a
> view to making its surroundings what they should be by means of
> certain decoration in houses—that is what I want to try to do.[45]

In a letter dated August 23, 1912, Ruth announced to Tudor-Hart her decision to abandon painting "as a means of expression," "for there are too many mediocre painters around," and she did not want to "encumber the world" with proof of her incompetence.[46] Ruth worked as an interior decorator in Paris, and both she and Owen scrimped on weekly expenses. They dreamed of living in Provence. Ruth was designing a home they planned to build themselves.[47]

Owen wrote frequently to his mother, with whom he had a close bond. Gertrude Merton was well-aware of his relationship with the American girl Ruth Jenkins but knew very little about Ruth herself. Gertrude's concerns were for her son's well-being and his career. She had concerns about Owen's ability to be married and financially stable. She was also threatened by the possibility that he would not return to New Zealand and that the bond she had with her son would be disrupted by his interest in Ruth.[48]

Ruth was aware of Owen's attachment to his mother and mindful that Gertrude Merton knew of Ruth only what Owen had communicated through his letters. Collins quotes from Ruth's letter to Gertrude of June 17, 1912:

> So that is why I want to write to tell you that, though I am only a
> very average girl, yet I have enough sense of the fitness of things to
> know that Owen deserves someone much better than I shall ever
> be. . . . You see, we were rather thrown together by circumstances
> after a long time when he had been working very hard and not
> meeting many girls socially at all and I was lonely too, so we were
> friends and discovered we liked a great many of the same things
> and had numerous common interests. Then this winter being at
> the studio together we saw each other all the time and that is how
> it happened.[49]

45. Collins, "Sense of Construction," chapter 8, 12.
46. Collins, "Sense of Construction," chapter 8, 20.
47. Collins, "Sense of Construction," chapter 8, 15.
48. Collins, "Sense of Construction," chapter 8, 21.
49. Collins, "Sense of Construction," chapter 8, 21.

Ruth presents as tactful, considerate, and clear-headed, not cold. Owen is "the dearest boy" she knows, "a manly lovable boy" whom she can look up to and "love just because he is so nice." She assured Gertrude that she had not yet accepted Owen's proposal of marriage for the following reason:

> It does not seem to me a man ought to be tied when he has several more years of study before he can marry, because he may develop and change a great deal in that time so that if he were engaged to a girl he had known only as long as we have known each other it might be a very terrible thing for him.[50]

Ruth, it seems, had already made up her mind regarding the marriage, but notice that according to her, the five-year delay was not for Owen's sake alone:

> I am afraid that if in five years he finds he still wants to marry me I shall not refuse . . . I think we might be very happy together. . . . Five years are a long time and we may both change very greatly before they are over. So in the meantime the only thing to do is to go on with our work to the best of our ability, and at the end of the time we shall be able to decide if we want to spend the rest of our lives together.[51]

Ruth's letter was intended to ease tensions and establish an appropriate relationship with the woman who would eventually become her mother-in-law. As Ruth and Owen's relationship became one that was now committed to marriage, Gertrude's concerns about money became more obvious.[52] Ruth attempted to reassure her that she and Owen would be financially secure, writing that she wanted to help Owen shoulder the responsibility for supporting themselves and a family:

> . . . to be free to paint by managing all the daily details . . . it is not being poor that we are on guard against, but being spoiled by being poor. . . I believe that one should earn one's dinner by good hard common labor, and one's dessert by one's art if the inspiration comes, and if it does not come, well then do without the dessert, but don't force either the inspiration nor the labor, to supply what it never was meant to supply.[53]

50. Collins, "Sense of Construction," chapter 8, 21.

51. Collins, "Sense of Construction," chapter 8, 21.

52. Collins, "Sense of Construction," chapter 9, 3.

53. Hempstead-Milton, "Merton's Search for Paradise," 10.

In a letter to Gertrude written in April 1913, Ruth wrote: "we are both strong and could work with our hands if we were in danger of starving."[54]

Owen reassured his mother that the relationship was deep, and he felt they were made for each other:

> We have struggled against each other in all kinds of ways. We have given in, in dozens of things, for the sake of getting nearer each other, so near to each other that I don't believe there are two other people in the world as near in their ideas and values as we are.[55]

As planned, in the summer of 1913, Ruth returned to America and to her family home in Douglaston, New York. She worked as an interior decorator and tried unsuccessfully to sell some of Owen's paintings.[56] After spending almost a year with her parents, Ruth returned to England. The passenger list of the liner SS *New York* lists R. Calvert Jenkins in first class, arriving from New York City to Southampton, England, on April 4, 1914.[57] A mere three days later she had taken the eighty-mile trip from Southampton to London and was married to Owen. The ceremony was performed on April 7, 1914, by the Reverend W. S. McGowan (Church of England) at St. Anne's Church, in the Soho neighborhood of London.[58] The witnesses were Gwynn Merton, Owen's sister (visiting Aunt Maud at the time), Aunt Maud and Uncle Ben Pearce, Tudor-Hart, and A. E. Atkinson (a painter from New Zealand who was a friend of Owen). Notably, no relatives of Ruth were present. The timing of the wedding, the manner in which it was conducted, and the absence of the bride's family raise questions that have little chance of being resolved satisfactorily since the people involved are no longer with us. The church records document the timing of the wedding, and Collins's impeccable research documents its conduct; however, neither provides an explanation of the reasons for the speed with which Ruth and Owen were wed once Ruth returned to England, nor reasons for some of the odd circumstances regarding the wedding itself. The third issue—the absence of Ruth's family—remains a matter of speculation, as does much of this event.

---

54. Hempstead-Milton, "Shared Facts, Different Stories," 41.

55. Collins, "Sense of Construction," chapter 10, 26.

56. Collins, "Sense of Construction," chapter 13, 10.

57. U.K. Incoming Passenger Lists (1880–1960).

58. England, Select Marriages (1538–1973).

Why such a hasty wedding? No legal issues appear to be relevant to the decision, there were no travel plans or schedules that had to be considered, and there was no chance of an unplanned pregnancy, as Ruth had been in the United States for nearly a year prior to the wedding.

The second question may be related to the first, but it is not possible to logically link the two without knowing more. Why Owen insisted that guests not be permitted inside the church is unknown.[59] While the ceremony was taking place, the guests waited outside the church under the trees. Whatever the reason, Owen's family and friends were not inside the church to view the wedding. Collins records they waited outside in the rain. Following the ceremony the group ate breakfast at the Eustace Miles Restaurant, where each guest paid for his or her own meal. Thence to Charing Cross Station, where Ruth and Owen began their journey to France.[60]

Ruth's parents, Sam and Mattie Jenkins, were not in attendance. They had the means to attend their daughter's wedding in London; further, as Sam was an executive with Grosset and Dunlap Publishing Company, he would have been able to take the time off necessary for the voyage to England and back. Although it is not possible to know with certainty, we may assume that Ruth's parents objected to Ruth's choice of Owen for her husband, for several reasons. First, as Owen was not known in New York, and his work had not yet generated any interest among buyers there, Sam and Mattie may have started to question his ability to provide for a wife, and later, for a family. A Midwesterner, Sam, who had been orphaned at age sixteen, had worked hard, eventually securing an executive position for himself in a thriving business. It may have been difficult for him to find Owen's chosen vocation, that of a Bohemian artist, as a responsible path for a man with a wife to support. Second, assuming Ruth talked about her courtship with Owen and their travels around France and Italy, it would have generated questions about sleeping arrangements, especially since her parents would have known Ruth's financial status. If it was known, through Ruth's admission, or if it was assumed, that the couple had premarital sexual relations, this would have rankled Sam in particular. An illegitimate pregnancy would have risked not only Ruth's social standing in her New York community, but Sam and Mattie's as well. Both were well-known in the Douglaston community, and Sam was on the vestry[61] of the church of

59. Collins, "Sense of Construction," Chapter 10, 27.

60. Collins, "Sense of Construction," Chapter 10, 27.

61. Church vestry: A group of elected parishioners, who, along with the rector,

which they were members, the Zion Episcopal Church; a premarital pregnancy would have placed Sam's position in jeopardy.

Whatever the issues that prompted the speed and the privacy of the ceremony, there was every likelihood of their marriage bringing them much happiness and mutual support. Both Ruth and Owen had been raised in families that valued education, culture, and music. Each of them followed a path into the arts, rather than into a professional career, as each of their siblings had chosen. Ruth's brother, Harold, was an engineer.[62] Owen's sister Beatrice (Ka)[63] was a nurse; sisters Sybil[64] and Agnes (Kit)[65] became teachers, while his older brother Llewyllen[66] became an attorney. Both Ruth and Owen were trained and talented artists who shared a love of music, theater, and dance. Ruth preferred interior design to painting and dedicated herself to support Owen's career. Ruth and Owen both had a Bohemian attitude toward life and opted for simplicity. There were no clear religious issues: both had been raised in the Anglican faith. They loved the culture of France and looked forward to settling into the local customs.

The chief stumbling block to their plans was the fact that they married without having the money or a solid financial plan about how to support themselves and a family. There is no clear record of whether they reached their goal of having a £300 annual income and £200 in reserve at the time of the marriage. What is known is that when they arrived in the village of Prades, in the Pyrenees Mountains of France they did not purchase land, nor did they build the house that Ruth had designed. Rather they rented two upper floors at Rue du 4 Septembre.[67] Sheila Milton,[68] an authority on Ruth, conjectured that, "It would seem to me that Ruth's idealism and Owen's naivete combined for tragic effects in their lives."[69]

---

manage the administrative and business affairs of the congregation.

62. U.S. School Yearbooks (1880–2012), *The Columbian* (1911).

63. New Zealand, Registers of Medical Practitioners and Nurses (1882–1933).

64. New Zealand, Teacher and Civil Service Examinations and Licenses (1880–1920).

65. "Personal Items," *The Press* (Feb 22, 1911).

66. New Zealand, School Registers and Lists (1850–1967).

67. Collins, "Sense of Construction," chapter 11, 12.

68. Sheila Milton, author and recipient of International Thomas Merton Society Shannon Fellowship (1999), has multiple publications about Thomas Merton and his mother Ruth to her credit.

69. Hempstead-Milton, "Shared Facts, Different Stories," 55.

The Merton Family in Prades

Prades is in the southwest corner of France in the Pyrenees-Occidentales in Southern France, on the border with Spain. It is part of Catalonia, which is a semi-autonomous region in northeast Spain. Set in the foothills of Mount Canigou, the landscapes are beautiful, and Prades enjoys a majority of days of sunshine each year. It attracts many tourists for hiking and mountaineering. Prades is known for its Pablo Casals summer concert, in honor of the Catalan cellist who lived much of his life in the town.

With the benefit of the tent given to them as a wedding gift by Tudor-Hart, Ruth and Owen spent the summer of their first year of marriage camping in Molitg, a village in the mountains four miles from Prades, where they painted.[70] It was Owen's hope to sell his paintings to the tourists. By the end of summer they rented an apartment on Rue du 4 Septembre.

Both Ruth and Owen acquired a basic closeness to nature, the land, and humble enjoyments that required neither money nor status. Ruth adopted the dress of the local inhabitants, Owen gardened barefoot, as did the locals, and they spoke French at home. Owen made furniture for the rooms of their home, and Ruth did the best she could on a limited budget to decorate. Owen remained hopeful that one day he could buy land, but it never happened. Owen sold a few paintings to tourists, adding to their meager income by playing the piano, possibly at the local cinema.[71]

Three months after their marriage, World War I began in July 1914. However unprepared financially they were, the outbreak of a world war could not have been foreseen. The effect on tourist travel in France was disastrous for Owen's sale of paintings. Although the battle lines in France were 600 miles northeast of Prades (Ruth and Owen were not in any real physical risk), tourism suffered, and Owen sold few paintings.

Collins does a credible job of clearly describing the situation at the time (he had access to French documents). There was no conscription of foreigners by the French government.[72] Foreign nationals were required to register at the town hall. If they did not appear at the town hall, they faced arrest due to fear they were involved in espionage. Owen had the choice of leaving the country or applying for a residential permit to remain in

---

70. Mott, *Seven Mountains of Thomas Merton*, 5.

71. Collins, "Sense of Construction," chapter 11, 13.

72. Collins, "Sense of Construction," chapter 11, 12.

France, providing he could prove he was able to support his family.[73] It would appear that there was no requirement to enlist; however, the government placed restrictions on foreign nationals so their whereabouts would be known. Ruth and Owen were able to maintain their residency in Prades, and Owen faced no criticism from the local people. In fact, he gave piano concerts in support of the war effort. He once gave a solo interpretation on the Allies' national anthems; his efforts were applauded in the local paper. [74]

After Tom was born, Owen wrote a letter dated January 10, 1916 to Esmond Atkinson, a friend and painter in New Zealand:

> We are ourselves some of the very few who are out of the trouble
> for the time being, and we are pretty selfish to be as we are, but we
> are selfish on account of little Tom chiefly, and so far as I do think
> I am worth more to Ruth and him than to the armies.[75]

Ruth was a pacifist influenced by her Quaker background (dating back to the late 1700s) and did not want her husband serving in the army.

Their first son, Thomas Merton, to be called "Tom" at Ruth's insistence, was born January 31, 1915. Neither Ruth nor Owen had ever been in the situation of taking care of children. Ruth, despite being unprepared for parenting, took on all the responsibilities of childcare. She took the role so seriously that she is known to have read every book she could find about child-rearing. When Tom was born, Ruth understood that her mother-in-law, Gertrude Grierson Merton, who was close to Owen, would want to know as much about her new grandchild as was possible. Ruth kept a journal recording each instance of Tom's growth and development, which she called Tom's Book,[76] and planned to send it to Gertrude. Ruth listed all his words, the objects that caught his attention, the food he ate, and the number of hours he slept. Tom was a child who:

> . . . kicked and screamed furiously when dressed or undressed . . .
> fought sleep always . . . never amused himself with toys . . . never
> would be rocked . . . never wanted to be held . . . rarely quiet a
> single moment when he is awake . . . was cross with strangers . . .

---

73. Collins, "Sense of Construction," chapter 11, 11.

74. Collins, "Sense of Construction," chapter 11, 13.

75. Furlong, *Merton: A Biography*, 10.

76. Merton, R., *Tom's Book*. Ruth created a similar book for John Paul, which is in a private collection and has not been published.

did not like people approaching him and screamed . . . slapped at people . . . refused to repeat words when asked.[77]

Tom himself recalled his early childhood as one in which he was, "stubborn . . . with unpredictable features . . . things she [Ruth] had never bargained for." [78]

Temperament is constitutional and part of the hard wiring each person has at birth. The significance of childhood temperament was not recognized until the 1956 New York Longitudinal Study results were published. This research showed that children are born with distinct temperaments that affect their attitudes and relationships, initially with parents, and then with others in their lives. Using a list of nine inherent traits, the child psychiatry researchers identified three groups of children: Easy, Difficult, and Slow to Warm Up.[79]

As an infant and child, Tom had many of the markers of the temperamentally Difficult Child. Parenting children like Tom is fraught with challenges and requires a parent to be structured in their discipline; otherwise, they will be manipulated by a demanding child. A new mother's attitude would understandably change after years of dealing with such a child.[80] Each person manages the characteristics of their own temperament over time and makes accommodations as they grow into the requirements of new stages of development.

Sales of Owen's paintings were not sufficient to support the family. Facing poverty in a French town during the war was not a viable option, so with the support and encouragement of her parents, Owen and Ruth decided to move to Ruth's family home in Douglaston, New York, at 50 Virginia Avenue. Apparently, no similar option existed with Owen's family in New Zealand; one reason may have been that the Merton family in New Zealand was not as financially stable as Ruth's family. It is possible, also, that Owen's family bore some hard feelings toward Ruth for preventing Owen from returning to New Zealand and toward Owen because he refused to serve in the military, whereas both his brother and cousin served during World War I.

77. Merton, R., *Tom's Book.*

78. Mott, *Seven Mountains of Thomas Merton,* 5.

79. Thomas et al., "New York Longitudinal Study, 1956–1988"; Chess and Thomas, *Temperament in Clinical Practice,* 28–41.

80. Mott, *Seven Mountains of Thomas Merton,* 17.

A little more than two years after marriage, all of Ruth and Owen's plans for how they would live were shattered. Both had shed themselves of the values of urban life with its style of dress and socialization to live a humble life of simplicity. The Jenkins family home, with its maid, cook, and housekeeper, was a very different lifestyle. This was a home and a place that contradicted many of the values that meant most to them. Owen had been independent in many ways since he was sixteen; becoming financially dependent on his father-in-law would have naturally implied a certain curtailing of his tendency toward bohemian ways. Even as an artist who may have assumed he would always need a patron, the idea of living under his father-in-law's roof and having to conform to the social and religious norms of that household must have been difficult to swallow.

Ruth and Owen left France with heavy hearts on August 5, 1916, but they never gave up hope of returning. Traveling in a first-class cabin with British passports, Owen, Ruth, and Tom left Bordeaux, France, on the liner SS *La Touraine*. The realities of war and the dangers of the voyage became clear to them as soon as they boarded, for the ship had been outfitted with guns on the decks for the dangerous trip across the North Atlantic.[81] The RMS *Lusitania* had been sunk by a German U-boat on May 7, 1915, eleven miles off the coast of Ireland. German submarines regularly patrolled the North Atlantic, so the danger was real. The Merton family arrived at the port of New York City on August 15, 1916,[82] sixteen days after the Black Tom explosion by German terrorists in New York Harbor that destroyed $20 million worth of weaponry destined for the Allied effort in Europe.[83] Ruth's parents, Sam and Mattie Jenkins, along with their son Harold, met their son-in-law Owen and grandson Tom for the first time at the dock. Owen not only greeted his well-to-do in-laws, but he also greeted a New York City skyline, the likes of which he had never seen. Both represented challenges to which he failed to adapt.

81. "Germans Unleash U-Boats."
82. New York, Passenger and Crew Lists (1916).
83. Federal Bureau of Investigation (FBI) History, "Black Tom 1916 Bombing."

2

Born into the Merton Family

SAFELY REMOVED FROM THE war and their poverty in a foreign country, Ruth and Owen initially lived with her parents. Owen had not enlisted for military service when he lived in France; in America, he was met with the required draft. As in France, he was able to avoid military service, but was required to make a declaration of his beliefs. His World War I draft registration card, dated June 2, 1917, stated an exemption as a conscientious objector as well as for being the sole support of a wife and child.[1] What price he paid in rejection and disapproval from his family, many of whom were in the New Zealand military, can only be guessed.

Ruth and Owen lived with Ruth's parents, Sam and Mattie Jenkins, beginning in August 1916. One can only wonder how the barefoot gardener and the daughter who wore peasant clothes adapted to a house with a maid, a cook, and a house cleaner. Eventually they acted on their need for independence and refused the largesse of the Jenkins family. Both struck an agreement that they would not ask Ruth's parents for money. Rejecting both a comfortable home and financial support, they struck out on their own. Sometime in 1918, they moved to a four-room house at 57 Hillside Avenue in Flushing, about five miles from the Virginia Avenue home of the Jenkins.[2]

---

1. U.S. World War I Draft Registration Cards (1917–1918).

2. Mott, *Seven Mountains of Thomas Merton*, 14.

1918 to 1921: Hope at Hillside Avenue

Ruth became pregnant with their second child in 1918, the year of the Spanish flu epidemic.[3] The most vulnerable people were those younger than five years of age and those between twenty and thirty years of age. The flu claimed 675,000 lives in the United States, of which 56,000 deaths occurred in New York state, and 20,000 deaths in New York City. Sam Jenkins worked in downtown Manhattan and traveled to and from his home in Douglaston each day. Living in the remote suburb of Manhattan on the western edge of Long Island probably contributed to their isolation, but the stress and fear would have been all-consuming, similar to the pandemic of 2020 and 2021.

Owen and Ruth had been in the United States for more than two years when John Paul was born on Saturday, November 2, 1918,[4] nine days before Armistice Day, November 11, 1918, marking the end of World War I. John Paul's New York City birth certificate shows Ruth Jenkins, thirty-one years old, as an unemployed mother, and his father, Owen Merton, as an artist of the same age. The family lived at 57 Hillside Avenue, in the Flushing neighborhood of Queens, with their first-born son, three-year-old Tom.[5]

John Paul Merton, 1918. Used with permission of the Merton Legacy Trust and the Thomas Merton Center at Bellarmine University.

3. "Spanish Flu."
4. New York, New York, Birth Index (1910–1965).
5. U.S. Federal Census (1920), Queens Assembly District 4.

As a baby, John Paul took his naps and had no temper tantrums.[6] He established a regular wake-sleep cycle early, was unruffled by changes of clothing or food, accepted the presence of strangers, and was not prone to crying or emotional outbursts. As Tom recalled:

> . . . he had a serene nature . . . a constant and unruffled happiness
> . . . when he was put to bed before the sun went down, he would
> lie upstairs, he was in his crib, and we would hear him singing a
> little tune.[7]

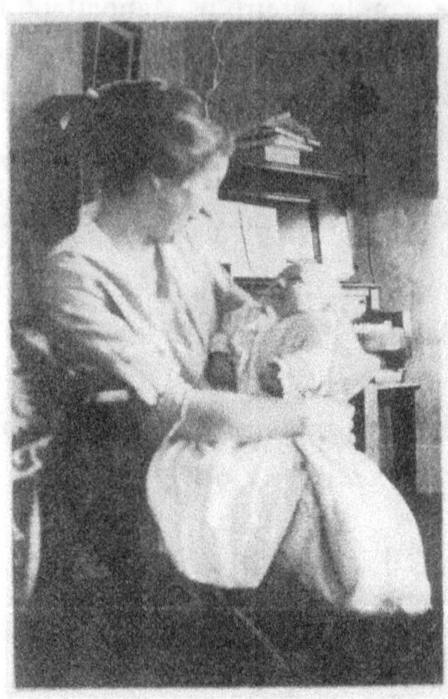

Ruth Merton holding John Paul, circa 1919. Used with permission of the Merton Legacy Trust and the Thomas Merton Center at Bellarmine University.

Comparison of the two brothers as babies was only natural for a mother. Ruth began to record John Paul's growth and development in a journal, as she had done for Tom. Her attention was now to be shared between the boys: Tom was no longer the center of her focus.

Tom's reaction to what he perceived as rejection was strong. Tom greeted his new brother with temper tantrums abundant enough for any number of children;[8] these tantrums blossomed into outright rejection in later years. Tom is seen in a family photo taken when John Paul was

6. Mott, *Seven Mountains of Thomas Merton*, 17.

7. Merton, T., *Seven Storey Mountain*, 8.

8. Mott, *Seven Mountains of Thomas Merton*, 17.

approximately one year of age.[9] Some authors report that in the photo, Tom is scowling.

Ruth holding John Paul with Tom in foreground, circa Spring 1919. Used with permission of the Merton Legacy Trust and the Thomas Merton Center at Bellarmine University.

Ruth maintained the small house into which John Paul was born. Tom recalled a memory of her while writing *The Seven Storey Mountain*: he remembered her "cleaning, sweeping, dusting with great energy and purpose."[10]

Ruth ran an orderly home.[11] The house was hardly more than a shack with four rooms, two on each floor, and a vegetable garden at the side of the house, and it was situated in an area of open space amid few houses.[12] She authored articles about living in a small house that described her ideas about the efficient use of space and multiple purposes for the rooms in an average house.[13] Ruth's ideas incorporated her knowledge of her Quaker background,

9. Mott, *Seven Mountains of Thomas Merton*, 19.

10. Merton, T., *Seven Storey Mountain*, 16.

11. Mott, *Seven Mountains of Thomas Merton*, 27.

12. Mott, *Seven Mountains of Thomas Merton*, 14.

13. Milton, "Introduction to 'The Tiny House,'" 9–17; Merton, R., "Tiny House," 182–85.

the interior decorating training she undertook in France, and her experience living in small houses in Prades and Flushing. The Quaker design principles favored simplicity, utility, and essentialism, and Ruth expressed them when she wrote, "many things we take for granted . . . can be quite well eliminated in our house."[14] She believed homes should reflect the needs of the family and contain only what was essential to the happiness of the family. Ruth advocated for rooms to be beautiful, no matter what function they served, and that a room should serve more than one purpose. "Let us make our kitchens attractive . . . they are not mere workshops . . . but the setting for some of our most cherished ideas and ideals."[15] She noted that kitchens in most homes were "about as attractive as the operating room in a hospital."[16]

Of the dining room, she wrote, "What we need is an out and out renaissance of all ideas on the subject of dining rooms,"[17] which she regarded as unnecessary. The dining room was to be "a real assembly room at mealtime or any other time when the family is together."[18] She was a proponent for an "other room" in each home as a "quiet place . . . not to be dispensed with."

> The other room may take many and various forms according to the tastes of the family. As a library, a salon, a music room or a study, it does duty both as a quiet place of retirement . . . it is not to be dispensed with if the tiny house is to be a success.[19]

The quiet place within each home was the place for meditation and creation, and for Ruth, perhaps a place in which to write.

Both Owen and Ruth's friends and acquaintances included literary people and people of the art world such as Bryson Burroughs, a neighbor and curator for the Metropolitan Museum of Art. However, they defied societal conventions: Owen befriended African American neighbors living nearby, as well as Black and Latino immigrants. Together, Ruth and Owen pursued a life of simplicity, accepted poverty, and eschewed the acquisition of unneeded possessions.[20] Ruth, raised in an affluent Episcopalian family, adopted a simple lifestyle as an adult. She was likely influenced by

14. Merton, R., "Tiny House," 184.

15. Merton, R., "Come into the Kitchen," 608.

16. Merton, R., "Come into the Kitchen," 608.

17. Merton, R., "Tiny House," 184.

18. Merton, R., "Tiny House," 184.

19. Merton, R., "Tiny House," 185.

20. Merton, T., *Turning Toward the World*, 177.

her mother, Mattie, who was raised within the Religious Society of Friends (Quakers), and with whom Ruth occasionally attended Quaker meetings. The Quaker values are integrity, equality, simplicity, community, stewardship of the earth, and peace, and members are guided by inner spiritual experience rather than rules.

Both Owen and Ruth were influenced by the French peasants in Prades. Owen continued to show a preference for "earthy" people and for the very earth itself, as he continued to work (barefoot) in his landscaping business.[21] Ruth preferred the simple peasant dress to those in vogue in New York and wrote admiringly of the simple, utilitarian homes of the French peasants.[22]

However serious Ruth was about interior decorating, she was more serious about being a mother. Ruth researched the most current information she could find about raising children. Ruth was concerned about:

> keeping the minds of their sons uncontaminated by error and mediocrity and ugliness and sham. . . ."[23] The boys were to be independent and have a character of their own, and not to be "an article thrown together in the common bourgeois pattern on everybody else's assembly line."[24]

Ruth's hope for their sons was that they would grow with a well-balanced and optimistic outlook on life.

John Paul was born into a family unlike the American family of the 1920s: his father *and* his mother pursued chosen vocations to support the family financially. Owen's passion was to devote his life to painting, but he started a landscaping business, based on what he had learned from the peasants in Prades, France.[25] He played the organ at the Douglaston Zion Episcopal Church for three years and earned a little money playing piano in the evenings at the movie theater in the nearby town of Bayside.[26] Although Ruth assumed primary responsibility for childcare and maintenance of the family home, as a talented interior designer, she continued to design and decorate homes for a few close friends after the birth of her children. In addition, she began to write and submit articles for publication

21. Hempstead-Milton, "Shared Facts, Different Stories," 47.

22. Merton, R., "Tiny House," 182–85.

23. Merton, T., *Seven Storey Mountain*, 9.

24. Merton, T., *Seven Storey Mountain*, 11.

25. Merton, T., *Seven Storey Mountain*, 14.

26. Collins, "Sense of Construction," chapter 12, 5.

devoted to her ideas about interior design, principally, that a home should be multifunctional to serve the needs of its residents.

While Ruth had accepted simplicity and poverty, it is doubtful that she accepted the depths to which they eventually sank. She had trusted that they could work their way out of poverty, remembering that her father rose from poverty to an executive position in a publishing house. However, it did not happen for Ruth as she hoped. Owen could not support his family with his art and landscaping, and he was unwilling to pursue other more lucrative employment.

Owen's paintings did not sell well, in spite of the help of his neighbor Bryson Burroughs, at the Metropolitan Museum of Art. Although Owen met people in the New York art scene, there were no financial benefits from these relationships. Owen's efforts were not able to establish financial security for the family. Owen saw the poverty the family was facing yet was unwilling to make the changes necessary to find work due to his passion for painting. Married with a growing family, he was temperamentally unwilling to shoulder family responsibilities.[27]

1921: A Mother's Letting Go

As 1920 rolled into 1921, the poverty of the little Merton family deepened, and life became more complicated by Ruth's illness. In 1920, Ruth was diagnosed with stomach cancer (according to her death certificate). They could not afford the medicine Ruth needed;[28] however, when Tom needed medicine, Ruth asked her mother for help, breaking her agreement with Owen not to accept money from her parents. Nevertheless, she persisted in the routine of her household work, did some interior decorating for families in New York City, and continued writing. Tom recalled his memory of this time in their lives: "How long she had been ill and suffering not without poverty and hardship, without our knowing anything of what it was, I cannot say."[29]

Owen had been corresponding with Tudor-Hart, his former painting instructor. In January 1921, he wrote:

27. Daggy, "Great Soul," 2–4.
28. Mott, *Seven Mountains of Thomas Merton*, 19.
29. Merton, T., *Seven Storey Mountain*, 14.

> . . . life is so damned complicated, it is next door to impossible to
> live and paint over here . . . I have been desperately determined
> to end this perpetual bondage of working long hours for a living
> wage . . . my wife is a brick [British, meaning a reliable person]
> who takes a good deal more than her fair share of worry and work
> . . . .[30]

One may ask why Owen let his sense of self-importance prevent him from asking for help from the Jenkins family. He did not appear to seek work from his brother-in-law, Harold, who, as an engineer, was likely to have contacts that may have provided manual labor work. Nor is there any record that Owen turned to his family in New Zealand for help. He had been sending his mother paintings from time to time, and she was very involved in supporting his career. Had she been asked for financial help, would she have offered assistance? No request was made. Owen's solution—unrealistic as it was—was to save money and return to France.

Ruth's illness, diagnosed in late 1920, worsened as 1921 progressed. Whether Owen recognized the extent or severity of Ruth's condition is unknown. He had to have known of the scarcity of food. It appears that Owen relied on Ruth's strength regardless of what he observed. There is no evidence that he changed his mind about the agreement he and Ruth had that they would not ask her parents for money.

Some have suggested the marriage was near its end. Not only was Ruth very ill, but the family was experiencing poverty the likes of which she had not ever imagined. Even food was becoming scarce, and she was not able to breastfeed John Paul. Sheila Milton noted "Ruth, we can safely assume, was able to feed her children even if she herself was not able to eat nor could she provide them with medical or dental care."[31] A Merton family member, in conversation with Sheila Milton, stated that Ruth, in the final months of her life, "withdrew from life in great bitterness and in an attempt to starve herself."[32] Stomach cancer makes the very act of eating a stressful, painful process. Whether or not Ruth's failure to eat was due to stomach cancer or some other reason, Owen must have noticed the significant weight loss Ruth had to have experienced. Speculation that Ruth committed suicide by not eating is doubtful at best, if not fundamentally wrong.

---

30. Merton, O., "'Owen Merton Letter,'" 10.

31. Hempstead-Milton, "Shared Facts, Different Stories," 41.

32. Hempstead-Milton, "Shared Facts, Different Stories," 37.

Ruth's illness progressed through the spring and summer of 1921. Dates for and the number of hospitalizations she experienced during that year remain unknown. By September 1921, Ruth had been admitted to a public ward at Bellevue Hospital in Lower Manhattan. Bellevue Hospital, an American institution at the forefront of medical innovation since the 1800s, was then, and remains still, an excellent hospital for both medical training and patient care. Ruth was not able to see her sons during her admission due to hospital policy; this suited her since she preferred that the boys not be exposed to the morbid aspects of life.[33] She was very attached to both her sons, as well as to her family of origin, and being alone in a public ward without seeing them would have been heartbreaking for her. Following her hospitalization in September 1921, neither John Paul or Tom ever saw or experienced their mother's loving presence again.

With Ruth's hospitalization, Owen was left with the responsibility of being father for the boys, as well as housekeeper, wage earner, and artist. He had already refused to live with his in-laws or take any financial help, but he was now overwhelmed. Despite his dislike of the Jenkinses' lifestyle, he decided to accept their help.[34] He moved into their home with his sons. How the Jenkins family handled this is also lost to history; one can only imagine the tension within the family. Sometime in 1921, Owen left the Hillside Avenue house with its garden and working-class friends for the comforts of the Jenkinses' Virginia Avenue home with an abundance of food and household help. Owen had believed this was a temporary move, that as soon as Ruth recovered, they would return to France as they had hoped. Ruth's recovery did not occur: the move to Virginia Avenue, temporary for Owen and Tom, became permanent for John Paul.

Before Ruth died, she wrote a note to be given to six-year-old Tom after her death, explaining that she would not see him again. Hospital rules, and probably her condition, prevented Ruth from saying goodbye to her sons in person. She wrote the note to Tom since this was the only means available to her of directly communicating with him.[35] It must have been a terribly emotional note to write to her son: she would not see him ever again. It is not known how John Paul was told. At almost three years old, John Paul would not be expected to comprehend his mother's death, or

33. Furlong, *Merton, A Biography*, 14.

34. Merton, T., *Seven Storey Mountain*, 14.

35. Thomas Merton described receiving this note at age six and the impact it had on him in his biography, *Seven Storey Mountain*, 14.

even recall the details in later life. If he had any memories of his mother, they would have been formed prior to his mother's hospitalization when he was about twenty-eight months of age.

Ruth's last hospital admission occurred on September 14, 1921; she died in Bellevue Hospital on October 3, 1921, at thirty-four years of age. The death certificate lists carcinoma of the stomach and colon with duration of one year as the cause of death, with intestinal obstruction of three days' duration as a secondary factor in her death.[36] At her request, Ruth was cremated and her ashes buried at the Fresh Pond Crematory and Columbarium in Middle Village, Queens.[37]

Ruth's life was lived according to the motto of her alma mater, Bradford Academy: "Surgo ut Prosim" (I rise that I might serve).[38] Her quiet service throughout her marriage to support Owen's painting career, and her fortitude in the last days of her life ring out loudly. The echoes of her sacrifice reverberate in the way John Paul lived his life and spent his last day. Poignantly, the first part of a two-part article Ruth wrote titled "The Tiny House," was published the same month of her death.[39]

Thus, the first three years of John Paul's life ended with the tragic loss of his mother, of which he had little comprehension. His mother was gone. The celebrations of his birthday and Christmas Day must have been somber.

Ruth's death had to be a crisis for the whole family. Her parents lost their daughter, her husband lost his wife, the bedrock of his stability, and the children lost their primary source of tenderness and love. The symbol for "crisis" in the Chinese language is the joining of two symbols: one for danger and one for opportunity. The time following Ruth's death was fraught with challenges for Owen, some dangerous and some opportunities. Owen interpreted the challenges of the crisis solely for his own benefit. It was for him an opportunity only to follow his passion to paint. Tom wrote, "Mother's death had made one thing evident. Father now did not have to do anything but paint."[40] Owen did just that. He also discovered new friends who would ultimately cause him further alienation from his in-laws, physical separation from John Paul, and emotional separation

36. New York City Health Department, Death Certificates.

37. New York, Extracted Death Index (1862–1948); Owen Merton is named as the person responsible for the expenses of the funeral on Ruth's death certificate.

38. "Campus History and Description."

39. Merton, R., "Tiny House," 182–85.

40. Merton, T., *Seven Storey Mountain*, 16.

from both sons. He avoided the financial and parental responsibilities and focused solely on his career. What he saw as opportunity ultimately turned into danger for his family.

Following his mother's death, John Paul would have been expected to spend more time with his father and his brother. As his core family, it was with them that he would be expected to grow, learn, and share his love of people. This was not to be.

3

A Life of Loss

PRIOR TO RUTH'S DEATH, Owen had been forced by necessity to move into the home of his in-laws. Owen had presumed this was a temporary arrangement until he could take the family to France, but Ruth's death altered that plan.

Recounting the life of John Paul's father and brother in the years following his mother's death gives clarity to the extent of the impact his mother's death had on John Paul's life and the family. The implications were profound. His would not have been a grief solely about the loss of his mother. His would also have been the sadness and confusion due to the cyclical loss and return of both his father and brother, without knowing why he was left or if they would ever stay with him. Vital and deepening attachments to both his father and brother failed to mature.

There were four instances when Owen left John Paul in the years following Ruth's death. A timeline showing Owen's travels after Ruth's death is presented below.

Table 2—Timeline of Owen's Departures from John Paul After Ruth's Death

Date	Travel
03 October 1921	Ruth Merton dies. John Paul and Tom left in Owen's care.
Winter 1921–22	Owen travels from Douglaston to Bermuda, leaving his sons at the Jenkins family home.
13 March 1922	Owen returns to Douglaston.

Date	Travel
July 1922	Owen and Tom travel to Provincetown, MA. John Paul remains in Douglaston.
August/September 1922	Owen and Tom return to Douglaston.
19 October 1922	Owen and Tom travel to Bermuda and stay with Evelyn and Cyril Scott. John Paul remains in Douglaston.
29 March 1923	Owen returns to Douglaston from Bermuda, leaving Tom with the Scotts in Bermuda.
26 April 1923	Evelyn and Cyril Scott travel from Bermuda to Douglaston, bringing Tom.
May 1923	Owen, Tom, and the Scotts travel to Buzzards Bay, MA and stay with Marie Garland and Swinburne Hale.
June 1923	Owen and the Scotts travel to Europe and Africa. Tom is left in Buzzards Bay with the Garland-Hales.
June 1923	Sam brings Tom from Buzzards Bay to Douglaston, reuniting him with John Paul.
29 June 1925	Owen returns to Douglaston.
28 August 1925	Owen takes Tom (age 10) to France. John Paul (age 7) will see Owen and Tom only on vacations from now until Tom is college age.

The first of Owen's departures occurred in the months immediately after Ruth's death in October 1921. The second occurred in the summer of 1922, and the third in October 1922. The third separation was to last from October 1922 (one year after Ruth's death) until June 29, 1925. The fourth separation happened in August 1925, when Owen moved to France, taking Tom with him and leaving John Paul permanently in the care of his maternal grandparents. By then, it was obvious that John Paul would not ever live with his father and brother, but that he would be raised by his maternal grandparents. One can imagine John Paul's grandparents struggling to answer their grandson's questions about his father's return when the boy was only six years old.

1921–1923: Bermuda and Buzzards Bay

From 1921 through 1923, Owen was influenced by two couples, the Scotts and the Garland-Hales.

Evelyn Scott (nee Dunn) and her husband[1] Cyril Kay Scott were literary people; each was a published author. They were supported by an allowance received from the millionaire couple, Marie Garland and Swinburne Hale, whose Buzzards Bay (Massachusetts) estate was managed by Cyril. In late 1921,[2] Evelyn Scott wrote to a friend, Lola Ridge, that she was "sending her" a man she had met, Owen Merton. Lola Ridge, a poet in New York City, was from New Zealand; presumably Evelyn Scott intended to make an introduction for Owen.[3] This letter suggests that Owen may have met Evelyn sometime in 1921 but there is not enough information to know whether this meeting occurred before or after Ruth's death. Exactly why or when Owen traveled to Bermuda is not known;[4] he returned from Bermuda in March 1922. The passenger list of the ship SS *Fort Hamilton* lists him on its return trip from Hamilton, Bermuda, to New York City on March 13, 1922.[5]

After a short visit in Douglaston, he left John Paul for the second time, taking Tom with him, to paint at an art colony in Provincetown, Cape Cod, Massachusetts.[6] On return to Douglaston, Owen stayed for an indeterminate time, and then, taking Tom and leaving John Paul again, went to Bermuda. The Garland-Hales owned a rundown mansion in Bermuda that Cyril Scott was renovating. On October 19, 1922, Owen and Tom went to Bermuda to help Cyril with the renovation of the mansion.[7] This was the third time in the months following Ruth's death that Owen, taking Tom with him, traveled away from New York, leaving John Paul behind.[8] There is the suggestion that Tom felt a sense of triumph at being chosen over his brother to go with his father.[9]

---

1. Some texts say it was a "common law" marriage; others say it was a legal marriage.

2. The letter quoted by Daggy ("Birthday Theology," 66), mentions that Owen's wife had just died; therefore, the letter had to have been written sometime after the date of Ruth's death, October 3, 1921.

3. Daggy, "Birthday Theology," 66.

4. Mott, *Seven Mountains of Thomas Merton*, 21.

5. New York, Passenger and Crew Lists (1922).

6. Merton, T., *Seven Storey Mountain*, 16.

7. Daggy, "Birthday Theology," 66.

8. Furlong, *Merton: A Biography*, 18.

9. Mott, *Seven Mountains of Thomas Merton*, 21.

When Owen's relationship with Evelyn became sexual isn't clear.[10] On March 29, 1923, Owen left Tom in Bermuda with the Scotts, who were veritable strangers to Tom (and whom Tom did not like) and went to an exhibition of his own work in New York.[11],[12] The reason Owen did not bring Tom back to his grandparents is unclear. Owen did not return to Bermuda. Later that month Owen wrote to the Scotts suggesting they come to Douglaston in mid-May.[13] It was possible they stayed surreptitiously in the Jenkinses' home because Sam, Mattie, and John Paul were absent, likely on a business trip of Sam's in Detroit. The Scotts returned from Bermuda to stay on Virginia Avenue, bringing Tom with them.

After meeting in Douglaston, the group traveled to visit the Garland-Hales at their home in Buzzards Bay.[14]

Drawing of Owen Merton by Maxwell Simpson in Buzzards Bay, MA, May 20, 1923. Used with permission of the Merton Legacy Trust and the Thomas Merton Center at Bellarmine University.

10. Collins, "Sense of Construction," chapter 13, 12.

11. Collins, "Sense of Construction," chapter 13, 17.

12. New York, Passenger Lists (1923).

13. Collins, "Sense of Construction," chapter 14, 1.

14. Collins, "Sense of Construction," chapter 14, 1.

Sometime during this period, the group made plans to go to Europe. Owen and the Scotts left Buzzards Bay for Europe in June 1923.[15] Owen had been deceptive with his in-laws about his relationship with Evelyn and it is not clear exactly when Sam and Mattie became aware of the truth. Once aware, Sam resented Owen's duplicity; Sam felt his financial support of Owen had gone to fund a scandalous affair.[16] When Owen left for Europe in June 1923, he did not return Tom to the Jenkins family; instead, Owen left Tom in the care of the Garland-Hales at Buzzards Bay. Owen may have been afraid to tell Sam and Mattie of the European painting trip. He may have been overwhelmed trying to handle Tom's behavior: Tom disliked Evelyn intensely and had outbursts of rage directed toward her. Owen may have left Tom with strangers (the Garland-Hales) as a punishment for Tom coming between himself and Evelyn.[17] Owen probably had multiple motivations for leaving Tom in Buzzards Bay; however, none of them reflect a father who understands the needs of his son. Tom must have felt abandoned. Daggy provided Tom's version of being left with the Garland-Hales family, as quoted from the unedited original version of the manuscript of *The Seven Storey Mountain*:

> I was such a wild, and noisy, and unpleasant little brat, that I was soon excluded from the dinner table and from the society of the lady of the house, and put with the Italian cook and the Negro maid and the other servants and I dare say I was even a penance to them . . . I found a checkbook lying around the house . . . wrote out a few handsome checks and sent them to the Montgomery Ward people in Chicago together with my order for all that I needed. [18]

Tom was found out and threatened with reform school; legal consequences were avoided when Marie Garland summoned Sam to take Tom to Douglaston in late June 1923.[19]

15. Daggy, "Birthday Theology," 74.

16. Daggy, "Birthday Theology," 78.

17. Daggy, "Birthday Theology," 74.

18. Daggy, "Birthday Theology," 75.

19. Mott, *Seven Mountains of Thomas Merton*, 25.

1923–1925: Brothers, Rivals, and Strangers

By Tom's own account in material edited from the original version of *The Seven Storey Mountain*, he had:

> . . . a total indifference to all standards of conscience. All I knew was that what I wanted was good, because I wanted it, and that what I did not want was evil because I did not want it. And my life consisted in getting the things I wanted, and avoiding the things I did not want; and the obstacles other people put in my way were simply something to be got around with patience and resourcefulness.[20]

The published version of this period in *The Seven Storey Mountain* simply said that at eight years of age Tom had "a selfishness unusual even in a child."[21] This description of John Paul's brother portends the nature of the relationship that would develop between them during John Paul's childhood: Tom's will prevailed; John Paul generally relinquished his own desires to appease his older brother. This dynamic set the conditions for the basis of their relationship, determining Tom's treatment of his brother through childhood and into adulthood.

Sam took Tom from Buzzards Bay back to Douglaston, where the relationship between the brothers was tested. John Paul and Tom lived together in their grandparents' home from June 1923 until August 1925, while their father traveled and painted with Evelyn and Cyril across Algeria and Europe.

John Paul regarded his brother with awe.[22] He wanted to be like Tom, and now he had the chance to tag along and do whatever Tom did. Sometimes the two brothers joined in adventures. They created trouble and confusion in the household; the instigator of their shenanigans is lost to history. They hid under the dining room table to annoy guests–particularly guests the boys disliked–or threw things into the dining room from the stairway landing.[23] They both went to the area in Douglaston where movies were being made and watched as W. C. Fields performed his slapstick scenes. They laughed and jeered.[24] John Paul was only too willing to follow his

20. Daggy, "Birthday Theology," 75.

21. Merton, T., *Seven Storey Mountain*, 14.

22. Forest, *Living with Wisdom*, 11.

23. Merton, T., *Seven Storey Mountain*, 22.

24. Merton, T., *Seven Storey Mountain*, 21.

brother's lead in having this kind of fun. Given these shared hijinks, John Paul understandably thought his brother was his playmate; instead, he was led into the role of troublemaker. The sibling rivalry that Tom had earlier expressed as temper tantrums blossomed into much more open rejection. For the most part, Tom regarded his brother as poor company.[25] To Tom, John Paul was a nuisance and not a playmate.

While the brothers lived with their grandparents, the Boyers family moved onto Virginia Avenue, a few houses down from the Jenkins.[26] Their two sons, Russ and Tommy, became friends with Tom and John Paul, respectively. Tom and Russ had a sort of gang that they formed with other boys in the neighborhood, and they built a clubhouse in the field behind the houses.

John Paul, wanting to be a part of his brother's life, tried to get into the clubhouse. According to Tom:

> We severely prohibited John Paul and Russ's little brother Tommy and their friends from coming anywhere near us. And if they did try to come and get into the hut or even look at it, we would chase them away with stones. When I think of that part of my childhood, the picture I get of my brother is this: standing in a field, about a hundred yards from the clump of sumaches where we have built our hut, is this perplexed five year old kid in short pants and a kind of leather jacket, standing quite still, with his arms hanging down at his sides, and gazing in our direction, afraid to come any nearer on account of the stones, as insulted as he is saddened, and his eyes full of indignation and sorrow. And yet he does not go away. We shout at him to get out of there, to beat it, and go home, and wing a couple of more rocks in that direction, and he does not go away. We tell him to play in some other place. He does not move. And there he stands, not sobbing, not crying, but angry and unhappy and offended and tremendously sad. And yet he is fascinated by what we are doing, nailing shingles all over our new hut. And his tremendous desire to be with us and to do what we are doing will not permit him to go away. The law written in his nature says that he must be with his elder brother, and do what he is doing: and he cannot understand why this *law of love* [italics added] is being so wildly and unjustly violated in his case.[27]

25. Merton, T., *Seven Storey Mountain*, 23.

26. U.S. Federal Census (1930), Queens, New York.

27. Merton, T., *Seven Storey Mountain*, 23.

This scene was replayed many times. Whether or not John Paul could recall the earlier temper tantrums of his brother, being excluded from the hut sent a clear message. His brother simply did not want him around. Instead of retaliating, crying, or tattling about his brother to his grandparents, John Paul did the unexpected: he kept it to himself and continued to reach out to Tom. For a five-year-old desperate to cling to his brother, John Paul consistently reacted in unexpected ways. Willing to endure almost anything to connect with Tom, John Paul took considerable risks.

John Paul and Tom in Douglaston, circa 1923. Used with permission of the Merton Legacy Trust and the Thomas Merton Center at Bellarmine University.

Because Tom and his friends thought of themselves as a true gang; they went one mile from their street to the clubhouse of a rival gang of boys, where they taunted them. One rainy day, Tom was at home with his friends, and they observed a large group of about twenty or twenty-five of these rather tough-looking boys from the rival gang gathered menacingly in the lot around the Jenkinses' house. The protection of the house was lost when the cleaning lady, Freda, ordered the boys to leave the house so she could clean. The boys ran out of the back of Tom's house and raced through the backyards to Bill Boyer's house. The gang remained in the street threatening a fight. Then, something happened, as John Paul:

> . . . came walking down the street with a certain . . . dignity and calm . . . he walked right into the middle of them and nobody even touched him. And so he came to the house where we were. We did not chase him away.[28]

The rival gang of boys left. This was the earliest of many similar actions that demonstrated John Paul's willingness to put himself at risk to protect others.

1925: Abandoned

It is not clear what prompted Owen to return from Africa after being away for more than two years. He sailed from Bordeaux, France, on the liner SS *Roussillon*, and arrived in New York on June 29, 1925.[29] Owen had lost some of his respectable luster during the past few years: he had lost weight and grown a beard; his overall appearance was unkempt. On first seeing his father, John Paul would not have recognized the bearded man disembarking from the ship.

When Owen arrived, he stayed with the Jenkins family at the vacation home in Ashuelot, New Hampshire. By this time, Sam was aware of Owen's affair with Evelyn Scott, and tried to persuade him to end the relationship. Owen announced to Sam and Harold, Ruth's brother, that he wanted to take both boys with him to France, to live with him and Evelyn. Sam and Harold both argued strongly against this. Sam was supporting Owen financially; he threatened to discontinue the funding if Owen continued to live with Evelyn while he had the boys with him.[30]

Why Owen did not think of his Aunt Maud or his sister Gwynedd, both of whom lived in London, as possible caretakers for the boys is a mystery. Personal correspondence to the author from John James Merton, a first cousin to John Paul living currently in New Zealand, mentioned family stories that suggest Owen's sisters were willing to help.

Owen took Tom with him to France, and left John Paul (not yet seven years old) with his maternal grandparents.[31] How Owen decided this course

---

28. Merton, T., *Seven Storey Mountain*, 24.

29. New York, Passenger and Crew Lists (1925).

30. Mott, *Seven Mountains of Thomas Merton*, 26.

31. Merton, T., *Seven Storey Mountain*, 29.

of action is a matter for debate. There is doubt about whether Owen even had the option of leaving both boys at the Jenkinses' home. It is conceivable that Sam, knowing how independent and mischievous Tom was, may have refused to allow his older grandson to remain in the Jenkinses' home without Owen present. Furthermore, if Sam wanted Owen to break off the relationship with Evelyn Scott, what better way than to insist he remain in Douglaston to parent his sons? If Sam tried to influence Owen's decision and force him to remain with his children, his effort failed. Owen and Tom sailed for France aboard the HMS *Majestic* and arrived in Southampton, England, on August 28, 1925.[32]

Owen's abdication of responsibility meant he chose between two options: his painting or his parenting; he chose his painting career. His choice resounded with implications for John Paul. Owen's inability to do what his children needed and his exclusive attention to painting were his tragic flaws. John Paul was left with his maternal grandparents. From the time his mother died in October 1921 until his father left for France in August 1925, a span of forty-six months, John Paul had lived with his father for approximately eight months. Now, as his father left for France with his older brother, John Paul became a veritable orphan and was never again to live with, or be cared for, by his father.

John Paul was left by his father in the hands of loving grandparents to make his way in the world, yet the message was clear: John Paul was not a significant part of his father's life. The cycle of separation and reunion, extending over four years, to which Owen expected his sons to adapt, placed John Paul, particularly, on an emotional rollercoaster, unable to form the attachment to his father he desperately needed, or to his brother, which John Paul desperately wanted. For the brothers themselves, the only time they would see each other from this time onward was on summer vacations until Tom returned from England where he had been in college.

John Paul suffered one insult after another to his developing ego in his first six years of life: loss of his mother, loss of his Hillside Avenue home, loss of his father, and the loss of his only sibling, Tom. Further, he had already endured rejection by his brother for reasons he was unable to understand.

Children need to make sense of their lives. Parents provide age-appropriate explanations so that what seems like chaos to their developing sense of reality can be experienced with calmness. Children usually seek these answers out from parents and can be comforted by the understanding they

32. U.K. Incoming Passenger Lists (1878–1960), piece 804.

bring. Absent this perspective, they still need to understand how to get by in the world. The alternative is to rely on themselves to puzzle it out. One possible explanation that occurs to them is that they must be doing something wrong for these bad things to happen to them. However, they have no idea what it is that they are doing wrong and cannot link their actions to their lives. Thus, some children develop a vague underlying sense that they are not good enough or that they are flawed in some way that they do not understand and cannot comprehend. The resulting plan then is to be in charge by trying very hard to do things correctly. They think, "Maybe if I do things just right, these bad things won't happen to me." They become very good at sensing what others need and trying very hard to do what will satisfy others. This plan conveys a heavy burden on their growing sense of self and limits its development. The underlying insecurity must be calmed before the child can explore his or her own needs. At times this becomes too great for them to continue so they opt for a plan to do whatever they like without regard for consequences they are unable to predict or control. Others develop a quiet sense of being overly confident in order to quell this fundamental insecurity and self-doubt. Most vacillate between these coping strategies.

We can only guess that John Paul finished his early childhood with something akin to this see-saw style of getting along in the world. We are left to ponder what might have been going on in the mind of a young boy who simply longed to be with those he loved. The law of love he was accustomed to had not been working. Parent and brother remained out of reach for unknown reasons. Yet John Paul kept reaching out and remained hopeful.

Reaching out to others becomes the mechanism by which the child reassures itself that all is well. This sociability has an overt signal that is positive and the insecure base from which it comes is rarely obvious. This sociability, the movement toward others, is characterized by a sensitivity to the needs of others. The child is then rewarded by satisfying the needs of others.

One might ask how a child with the degree of loss and neglect that John Paul experienced establishes any sense of hope for himself. Certainly, John Paul's temperament contributed to his ability to cope. He was an "Easy Child"[33] who usually had a positive mood, adapted to new situations readily, and had a calm nature. But that is not the whole story. Temperament is just the constitutional base upon which experience builds a personality. His

33. Chess and Thomas, *Temperament in Clinical Practice*, 28–41.

early experiences with his grandparents would have opened his eyes and heart to a loving relationship. Certainly, his grandmother's practical nurse and companion, Elsie Hauck, was a warm and attentive presence in his life. One can speculate that John Paul saw his grandfather as a success in life and could relate to Sam's being an orphan at a tender age. John Paul formed attachments to those positive folks and experienced some sense of security. Yet hope was elusive for him. He did not yet have the cognitive ability to see all the possibilities of his future life. Nor could he embrace the unknown and unknowable with any sense of trust that his needs for a father would be satisfied. He could only experience the present fact that his father had once again left him. He had every reason to be sad, profoundly sad.

4

Childhood in Douglaston

Belonging

JOHN PAUL WAS A member of the Jenkins family for some time without knowing if this would be permanent. When his father left New York in August 1925, John Paul was six years old and became a permanent member of the Jenkins household. His grandparents were eager to compensate for the loss of his mother and the years of privation. They were also aware of how little time John Paul had spent with his father, and they devised a plan to help him cope with the separation from his father and brother. The plan was that John Paul, his grandmother, and grandfather would travel to Europe every two years to visit his father and brother, thus maintaining some semblance of attachment to them.[1] The first of these trips was planned for the summer of 1926.

John Paul's uncle, Harold Jenkins (Ruth's younger brother, thirty-six years old), had designed and built the Jenkinses' family home at 50 Virginia Avenue (now Rushmore Avenue) in Douglaston, in the borough of Queens, New York.[2] At that time Douglaston was a newly developed, upper middle-class suburb of Manhattan in the northwest corner of Queens. The Jenkinses' household was a social and happy place. John Paul's grandparents loved him dearly, and his Uncle Harold enjoyed playing with him. In

1. Mott, *Seven Mountains of Thomas Merton*, 63.

2. Mott, *Seven Mountains of Thomas Merton*, 14.

addition to his grandparents and his Uncle Harold, the household boasted a cleaning lady, a cook, and a German maid, Freda Schnell, who lived with the family.[3] There were several dogs to play with and woods in which to run. The ice box was always filled with food and there were more than enough magazines and comic books to read.[4]

Sam was a self-made man who worked as the Publicity Manager for Grosset and Dunlap Publishers on Twenty-Sixth Street and Broadway in Downtown Manhattan. Sam was on the vestry of the Douglaston Zion Episcopal Church; however, his true church was the local movie house where he saw every movie that came out. Both he and his wife Mattie loved the movies, and it was impossible to live in their house without catching their fascination with them.[5] He particularly liked W. C. Fields and Charlie Chaplin. He was a loud and bombastic person who would command the attention of those in any room into which he walked by slamming his folded newspaper on a table and barking questions or orders. He was exuberant, full of life, and controversial. He disliked Catholics, Jews, and African Americans, and his opinions were the subject of dinner conversation.[6] He belonged to the Masonic Order of Knights Templar. Sam and Mattie held frequent dinner parties and enjoyed the company of their neighbors. Sam could whistle opera tunes while Mattie accompanied him on the piano.

Mattie was quiet and retiring, the opposite of her husband. Prior to their marriage she had been bookkeeper for her sister Lizzie's husband, Roger Ebert, who owned a Fancy Goods shop.[7] In any social or family setting, as Sam became louder, she became more reticent. She did not lead the family overtly but could make her opinions known when needed. She was the peacekeeper during heated discussions at the dinner table. Mattie had a kiln in which she fired china after painting it first by hand.[8] Her hometown of Zanesville had a large factory where pottery was manufactured, and she may have picked up the hobby of painting china early in her life. She was an unpretentious, humble woman who enjoyed the arts, travel, and the many guests they entertained. Mattie had diabetes[9] and was frequently

3. New York State Census (1925).

4. Merton, T., *Seven Storey Mountain*, 396.

5. Merton, T., *Seven Storey Mountain*, 22.

6. Merton, T., *Seven Storey Mountain*, 25.

7. U.S. City Directories (1822–1995).

8. Merton, T., *Seven Storey Mountain*, 14.

9. Mott, *Seven Mountains of Thomas Merton*, 16.

ill but had the help of a companion, Elsie Hauck (later, Elsie Holahan), for many years. Elsie probably also cared for John Paul. Although Elsie cared for members of the Jenkins family, it is unknown if she actually resided within the home itself.

Elsie Hauck married Patrick J. Holahan in May 1917.[10] Patrick Holahan had been a captain in the Irish Volunteers and participated in the Easter Rebellion of 1916.[11] In 1920, Elsie lived on Sixty-First Street in Brooklyn, in her parents' home, with her husband and two children, and the U.S. Federal Census that year listed her as having no occupation.[12] The New York State Census of 1925 places her living in North Hempstead with her husband, Patrick J. Holahan (head of household), their two children, Patricia and Peter, her parents, Peter and Frieda Hauck, as well as her brother, Walter Hauck.[13] At this time her occupation was reported as "Housework." In 1930, the Federal census reported Elsie Holahan living with her parents (Peter Hauck, her father, was listed as head of household), her two children, and her brother Walter.[14] Her husband, Patrick Holahan, is not mentioned in the census record. Using various resources on Ancestry.com, no record for Patrick Holahan was located for the years following the 1925 Federal Census. In the 1930 Federal census, Elsie's occupation was listed as "Practical Nurse." The sudden appearance of Elsie's new occupation probably results from her work as companion to Mattie Jenkins, which likely was a necessity as a result of her husband's presumed abandonment.

John Paul began his education at five years of age in September of 1924 (he turned six years old two months after beginning the school year). The decision about the school he would attend was made by his grandparents and not his father. For elementary school, John Paul first attended PS 98, the neighborhood public school a few blocks from his house.[15] Later, he attended The Choir School of the Cathedral of St. John the Divine, an all boys' school (John Paul's Uncle Harold had also attended The Choir School).[16]

10. New York, Marriage License Indexes (1907–2018).

11. U.S. World War I Draft Registration Cards, New York (1917–1918).

12. U.S. Federal Census (1920).

13. New York Census (1925).

14. U.S. Federal Census (1930).

15. Ottawa, Canada, Library and Archives, "WWII Service Files of War Dead (1939–1947)."

16. St. John the Divine is an Episcopal church and the Cathedral church of the Episcopal Diocese of New York, meaning a church that is also the seat of a Bishop. Construction of the Cathedral began in 1892, making it over 125 years old. St. John is the largest

When PS 98 was demolished in 1930 (the school was likely demolished due to a fire),[17] John Paul attended The Choir School for the academic year 1929–1930 (the 1930 Federal Census reports John Paul as a student at The Choir School of the Cathedral).[18] PS 98 was rebuilt, now located at 4020 235th Street in Douglaston.

Prior to attending The Choir School, John Paul was baptized at Zion Episcopal Church on 29 June 1929, by the Reverend Lester Riley. Although the church has a record of the baptism, no baptismal certificate could be located. John Paul had not been baptized as an infant. His grandparents, anticipating his enrollment at The Choir School, had him baptized in the summer before the academic year started, as baptism was required for enrollment. The following year, he was among a group of seventeen students from The Choir School to be presented for confirmation on April 17, 1930. It is likely that he completed his elementary school years at The Choir School during the academic year 1930–31. The student records of PS 98 were lost in the fire sometime in 1929; there were no student attendance records kept for The Choir School, according to Wayne Kempton, the archivist for the Episcopal Diocese of New York (personal correspondence to the author, August 20, 2021). In 1941, on his application for enlistment in the Royal Canadian Air Force (RCAF), John Paul listed PS 98 as the only elementary school he attended.[19] There is no mention of the Choir School, yet his attendance at the Choir School is documented by his confirmation record and census record. At the time John Paul applied for admission to the RCAF, he may have recorded on the application the name of the school he attended for the longest period of time.

1926–1928: Summer Vacations in Europe

1926

In the late spring of 1926, almost nine months after leaving Douglaston, Owen's contentment with his new home in St. Antonin, France, and his

---

Gothic Cathedral in the world. Measured by length or internal volume, it is one of the five largest church buildings in the world.

17. PS 98Q-The Douglaston School, "PS 98 School History."

18. U.S. Federal Census (1930).

19. Ottawa, Canada, Library and Archives, "WWII Service Files of War Dead (1939–1947)."

painting were interrupted by news from his father-in-law that Sam and Mattie, along with John Paul, would be visiting during the summer months. This was to be their first biennial trip as planned by Sam. Although the difference in values and lifestyle played a part in Owen's irritation at news of this visit, an additional reason was the itinerary Sam had planned. Rather than bring John Paul to St. Antonin where he might share some relaxed time together with his father and brother, which had been the intent of these visits, Sam planned a two-month tour of England, France, and Switzerland. Sam had not consulted Owen about the plan, instead telling him to meet in Paris for a whole-family tour of Switzerland. The plan was to return from Switzerland to stay for a period of time in St. Antonin. Sam probably thought that because he was paying for this vacation, Owen would be pleased, but Sam often didn't realize how others felt. Owen preferred to be painting rather than touring and he referred to these visits as "invasions."[20]

The dynamics of this three-generational family were played out during this trip, displaying their dysfunctional relationships, and resulting in nervous exhaustion for all.[21] In fact, the trip was so imprinted on Tom's memory that he devoted almost five full pages to it in his autobiography. It is from that account that most of the details are known and described herein. In describing it, he could not list all of the places the family argued but fight they did.

The passenger list of the White Star Line ship, the RMS *Majestic*,[22] shows Sam, Mattie, and John Paul staying in a first-class cabin for the five-day ocean voyage. The *Majestic* was the world's largest ship, and its luxurious accommodations were eye popping for John Paul. On June 11, 1926, the *Majestic* deposited them and sixteen pieces of luggage (Sam had a difficult time keeping organized) in Southampton, England, on June 11, 1926.[23] This was John Paul's first time outside of the United States. One can only imagine the reactions of a young boy of seven years of age boarding this ocean liner and crossing the North Atlantic. He would have had many questions, or even fears, that both Sam and Mattie would have been able to answer. Sam and Mattie had already taken a similar trip after their daughter

20. Merton, T., *Seven Storey Mountain*, 44.

21. Merton, T., *Seven Storey Mountain*, 47.

22. RMS is an abbreviation for Royal Mail Ship (sometimes also steamship or steamer). It is the ship prefix used for seagoing vessels that carry mail under contract to the British Royal Mail.

23. U.K. Incoming Passenger Lists (1878–1960).

Ruth graduated from Bradford Academy, and they had experience from which they could offer reassurance and answers.

Once in Europe, John Paul, anxious to see his father and brother, had to wait, as the first item on Sam's agenda was a tour of London. They stayed in the grand Cecil Hotel and visited as many sights as Sam could schedule, before heading to Stratford-upon-Avon and then The Cotswolds. Next, the family of three went across the English Channel to France and the Loire valley. Sam embarrassed Mattie, Tom, and John Paul by throwing coins out the window of the tour bus and laughing, along with the other American tourists, while the children scampered to get the money. On this trip, John Paul visited Orleans, Nantes, and the Château de Chenonceau, Blois, and other estates in the region.[24]

Next, it was on to Paris, where Sam booked rooms in the Continental, one of the most expensive hotels in the city. By the time Owen and Tom got there, John Paul was in a bad mood, as was Mattie, due to Sam's boisterous performances along their route. Both had been opposed to his behavior on the bus, tossing coins along the road. As Tom recounted later, both he and John Paul realized that many people were laughing at Sam and not with him, and that by association with him, John Paul and Mattie may also have been judged as crude and lacking in social graces.

This was the first time the group had been together in some time. Sam approached the hotel bellboys with assertive orders about how to handle the mountain of luggage they had with them, the staff of restaurants with a snap of his fingers and a wave of hand to get quick service, and the museum clerks with irritation when they could not speak English. Sam's brash, ostentatious behavior appalled Owen, who had assimilated French culture and its diversity. The tension was exacerbated by the knowledge that Owen was still involved with Evelyn Scott, his married lover, despite having told Sam that he would end the relationship. Sam and Owen's polite veneer quickly dissolved, and bickering broke out frequently.

In Switzerland, several events occurred which brought to the surface all the uneasiness of the visit. The family was without a German language translator so they had a difficult time getting from place to place, nor could they read the museum item descriptions very well. Both John Paul and Tom coped by making fun of it all and putting their hats on statues and busts of famous Germans, which the museum guides did not take well. The family tension reached a critical juncture during the ride on the rack

24. Merton, T., *Seven Storey Mountain*, 45.

and pinion Jungfrau Railway to the mountain top, when Owen and Sam argued about the exact height of the Jungfrau mountains. Tom named this day the worst day of the whole visit.[25] On another day John Paul walked outside into the blinding field of white snow without his sunglasses and got a bad headache. It was in the lobby of an Interlaken hotel that John Paul humiliated the whole family by falling fully dressed into a pond of goldfish and running through the hotel dripping with water and green weeds. Was he just a spunky kid, or did his brother, with a wink and a nod, put him up to it? After all, it was a boring excursion for the eleven-year-old Tom, who was almost four years older than John Paul. For John Paul, mixed with the thrill of sightseeing was the disappointment of not being emotionally closer to his father and brother.

The dynamics of this troubled family were on full display at one point in the hotel at Lucerne, when Tom stated that the Americans stole the tune of "God Save the King" for the anthem known in the United States as "My Country, Tis of Thee." Tom and John Paul argued about this, almost coming to blows. Tom took the side of Great Britain, and John Paul defended the American point of view. Mattie agreed with John Paul. It is not known who started this argument, but it expressed the tension palpable at this family reunion, a gathering Owen had not wanted.

From Switzerland, the family went to Owen's home in St. Antonin, France. According to Tom, Sam thought the streets of St. Antonin were dirty; he wanted to leave as soon as possible.[26] Mattie insisted that they stay for the time they had planned, so Sam allowed them to stay long enough to go to Montauban, to visit the Lycée Ingres, the boarding school that Tom was to attend in the fall (the tuition was paid by Sam). John Paul and his grandparents left Cherbourg on August 19, 1926 on the SS *George Washington*, arriving in New York on August 27, 1926.[27]

It was done. The first of the biennial "vacation" trips John Paul was to take had left him exposed to many cultural and historical sights. His education outside the classroom had been a success; however, his connection with his father and brother left much to be desired. What had been imagined to be an opportunity for family bonding, especially for the two boys, only resulted in memories of strife and irritation. Most of the time was spent

25. Merton, T., *Seven Storey Mountain*, 47.

26. Merton, T., *Seven Storey Mountain*, 48.

27. New York, Passenger and Crew Lists (1926).

bickering and arguing.[28] Other than the bit of fun mocking the statues and paintings in the Swiss museums, the trip had been one long altercation.

1928

Nearly nothing is known of the circumstances of Owen and his sons during the summer of 1927. In June 1928, Owen, taking Tom with him, (Tom was thirteen years old), left St. Antonin and went to live with his Aunt Maud and her husband Ben Pearce at 18 Carlton Road, Ealing, West London.[29] Ben was a retired schoolmaster and his sister-in-law, Mrs. Robert Pearce, a widow, was Headmistress at Ripley Court Preparatory School, in Surrey, where Tom was later enrolled.

The move from St. Antonin occurred because of Owen's inability to support himself and Tom. Owen's former teacher Tudor-Hart had offered him an allowance of £100 a year if Owen would give Tudor-Hart first choice of Owen's paintings each year. Also, both Aunt Maud and Sam Jenkins offered to help with Tom's education. It seems that Maud and Sam shared the cost. Owen accepted.[30] All these factors boiled down to a single issue: Owen was still unable to support himself and his family.

Apparently, Owen and Tom made their home with Aunt Maud for the remaining months of the summer of 1928. Owen and Tom traveled to Rye, Canterbury, Romney Marsh, and Bodiam Castle, in East Sussex, and later, to France. [31] When school began in the autumn of 1928, Tom went to Ripley Court, where he boarded, and Owen left to pursue his painting. In the fall term of 1929, Tom transferred to Oakham School, at Uncle Ben's recommendation.

In the summer of 1928, the second biennial trip to Europe for a family visit was to have occurred; however, there is no record of Sam and Mattie, together with John Paul, meeting or connecting to Owen and Tom. Further, there are no details to explain why father and sons were not reunited, even briefly. Possibly, Owen so objected to Sam orchestrating the visits that he simply ignored the invitation. Sam may not have communicated his plans to Owen or there may have been some failure to the communication method—a telegram not received, for example. In any event, both families

28. Mott, *Seven Mountains of Thomas Merton*, 36.

29. Merton, T., *Seven Storey Mountain*, 60.

30. Mott, *Seven Mountains of Thomas Merton*, 40.

31. Mott. *Seven Mountains of Thomas Merton*, 48.

were on the same continent at the same time, but no source was found confirming that they met. How John Paul made sense of this is not known.

Passenger list records show Sam, Mattie, and John Paul sailed from New York to London on the SS *Minnewaska*, arriving July 23, 1928.[32] There are no records of where Sam, Mattie, and John Paul traveled, or of them meeting Owen and Tom. Mattie and John Paul returned home, leaving from Liverpool on October 13, 1928, on the SS *Adriatic*, and they arrived in New York about eight days later.[33] The details of Sam's return are not known, and it is not known why John Paul missed the first two months of the school year.

The return home for John Paul meant going back to life on Virginia Road. He probably had great stories to tell when asked by his teacher for a description of how he spent his summer. Like most New York City kids, he would have played baseball, stickball, box ball, scully,[34] Ace/King/Queen,[35] and other street games. There were butterflies to add to his collection, and stamps to fill his stamp book.[36] He wanted to be a scientist,[37] no doubt due to the influence of his Uncle Harold, the engineer. He returned to the stability of life with his grandparents.

Orphaned

1930–31: A Father's Dying

Four months before his twelfth birthday, John Paul took his third trip to Europe to visit his brother and father. He sailed with his grandparents on the SS *Minnewaska*, arriving in London on July 14, 1930.[38] This summer trip of 1930 was subdued because of the stock market crash and the economic depression of 1929; these events took a toll on the entire world. Fortunately, Sam had been a wise investor, purchasing property in addition

---

32. U.K. Incoming Passenger Lists (1878–1960).

33. U.K. Outward Passenger Lists (1890–1960).

34. Scully is a game played with bottle caps. A square is drawn with chalk, and the goal is to get the bottle caps into all 4 corners and the center circle.

35. Ace/King/Queen is a ball game played with at least 3 players; the goal is to eliminate your opponents.

36. Merton, T., *Seven Storey Mountain*, 397.

37. Merton, T., *Road to Joy*, 57.

38. U.K. Incoming Passenger Lists (1878–1960).

to making other financial gains. Grossett and Dunlap was still in business; he survived personal financial ruin. However, the future was unpredictable, and because Sam was thoughtful about the financial stability of his family, his thoughts turned to the financial future of both his grandsons. Before the vacation trip of 1930, he set up trust funds that would support both Tom and John Paul, at least through their college years.[39] During the trip, Sam told Tom of his plans for their financial security.

Owen Merton was hospitalized in August 1929, at Middlesex Hospital in London, England, under the care of his childhood friend, Dr. Thomas Bennett. Owen had brain cancer. His hospitalization included several unsuccessful surgeries, and there was no hope of survival. Before making the trip to London, Sam must have known that Owen was in the hospital in serious condition.[40] Owen understood that his illness was terminal, so he made a will on July 24, 1930. In the will, he appointed Sam Jenkins and Tom Bennett as guardians for his sons, John Paul and Tom, respectively. Sadly, it appears that Owen, who traveled alone or with the Scotts through Africa and Europe when the children were younger, considered their welfare only when faced with his own death. Had Sam and Mattie suffered severe illness or death during his travels, both children could have become wards of the state.[41]

When Sam and his family arrived in London, first, they went to Oakham, where Tom was in school, staying at the Crown Hotel.[42] Next, they went to London to visit Owen in the hospital. It was a quiet visit. Most of the time, the family stayed in London so they could be near the hospital to visit Owen.[43] There, John Paul saw his father for the first time since the 1926 vacation trip. Despite age limitations for children imposed by the hospital, John Paul was able to visit his father. This was probably due to the fact that Owen's doctor was his childhood friend, Dr. Bennett, who as dean of the Middlesex Hospital Medical School[44] probably gave his permission for this exception. For John Paul, this hospital visit was much worse than seeing his father with a beard and looking unkempt, as when Owen returned from Bermuda in 1925. Owen had been a virtual stranger

---

39. Merton, T., *Seven Storey Mountain*, 77.

40. Collins. "Sense of Construction," chapter 17, 7.

41. Collins, "Sense of Construction," chapter 17, 11.

42. Merton, T., *Seven Storey Mountain*, 77.

43. Merton, T., *Seven Storey Mountain*, 81.

44. Trail, "Thomas Izod Bennett."

in his life, but what this eleven-year-old boy saw in the hospital would have been emotionally wrenching. His grandparents would have tried to prepare him for his father's appearance: his father's face swollen, his eyes clouded, his forehead swollen and disfigured. Owen could not speak but understood their conversation and had a clear mind.[45]

Tom broke down and wept at his father's hospital bedside. Watching his brother's reaction must have been excruciatingly painful for John Paul. John Paul was witness to his father's suffering, the hopelessness of the situation, and his brother's sorrow. These experiences must have intensified his own feeling of helplessness. The family went to the hospital once or twice a week during the entire summer.[46] There was nothing they could do except be present and maintain a vigil.

There exists no record describing John Paul's thoughts and feelings about his father during this time. One can only speculate that his expectations about visiting Owen in 1930 were severely disappointed, and that any hopes he had for a meaningful relationship with his father were destroyed. What had he anticipated? What had he wanted to say to his father? Perhaps he planned to tell Owen about attending the Choir School, and that he had been confirmed at the Cathedral of St. John the Divine a few months prior. Perhaps he admired the drawings his father was making while in bed. Did he sit at the bedside in silence, grappling with feelings about a father with whom he had only lived eight months in a total of nine years since his mother's death?

It is not known if other Merton family members also came to support Owen, or if they were present when John Paul was there. Owen's sister, John Paul's Aunt Gwynedd, and her husband, Erwin Trier, lived in Fairlawn, Cranmore Lane, Surrey, thirty-six miles from the hospital. Aunt Maud, his mother's sister, lived about ten miles from the hospital, on Carlton Road in Ealing, West London, with her husband Ben Pearce. Maud had a reputation in the family for being a sensitive and loving person and she would have had kind words and been a support for John Paul and his grandparents.

It would have been a sad leave-taking when John Paul had to go home to Douglaston. Sam sailed by himself from Plymouth and arrived in New York on August 12, 1930.[47] Mattie and John Paul left from London on

45. Merton, T., *Seven Storey Mountain*, 82.

46. Furlong, *Merton: A Biography*, 46.

47. New York, Passenger and Crew Lists (1930).

August 30, 1930, and arrived in New York on September 8, 1930.[48] That the family returned to the United States via two separate trips is curious: possibly Sam needed to return to his job, yet both grandparents wanted John Paul to have as much time as he could with his father, and so Mattie lingered in London with John Paul. Tom stayed at Oakham School for the rest of the year and visited his father frequently.

When John Paul's mother died, he was not yet three years old and had little awareness or understanding of anything except the fact that she was gone. He did not know why she had left him or if he would see her again. Gradually, her absence became his reality. John Paul was nearly twelve years old while his father lay dying in a London hospital; he had some understanding. Yet, the physical separation—he was in Douglaston, his father in London—left him feeling helpless and profoundly sad. He left the hospital without any sense of closure about his father and his feelings about Owen's anticipated death. At age twelve he spent the winter of 1930 confused about one of the fundamental issues of life: death. He was alert during these months for any news of his father's condition. Whether by phone or telegram, the news came that his father died on January 18, 1931, at the age of forty-three years.[49] John Paul was told by his grandparents, who were caring and sensitive. His Uncle Harold would have been supportive and consoling. It is not known why the Jenkins family, including John Paul, did not go to the funeral. It is likely that there was not sufficient time to travel to England. Owen was cremated at the Golders Green Crematorium in London, and his ashes scattered there.[50]

Tom was present at the funeral, as were Maud and Ben Pearce, Erwin Trier, Mr. O. Theiss, Mr. F. R. Ford, and Mr. and Mrs. Percyval Tudor-Hart were in attendance, as well as Owen's doctor and friend, Dr. Tom Bennett and his wife.[51] Owen's name was inscribed in the Waimairi Cemetery, in Canterbury, New Zealand.[52]

Without a fully developed cognitive capacity, boys of John Paul's age have some understanding of death but do not have the ability for the abstract thought necessary to absorb the full emotional effects of the death of a parent. Grief can take many forms, and we can only imagine the way John

48. New York, Passenger and Crew Lists (1930).

49. "Obituary: Owen Merton."

50. Collins, "Sense of Construction," chapter 17, 11.

51. Collins, "Sense of Construction," chapter 17, 11.

52. "Owen Heathcote Grierson Merton."

Paul processed the death of his father. He would have been ambivalent, i.e., having contradictory feelings about the same thing at the same time. On the one hand, he had little relationship with his father. They had spent little time together, and when his father left him, there seemed to be no explanation as to the reason. On the other hand, Owen was his father whom he was supposed to love, yet this emotion was stifled by repeated absences and the feeling of abandonment. The loss of his father was not the loss of past memories but the loss of any possibility of creating future memories or a relationship with him. Bereft of any eventual attachment to his father, he would have experienced a sadness of the emptiness of both past and future. His grief would have been muted by ambivalence. He was left to establish his identity as a teenaged boy with a new word to identify him: orphan. None of his friends were orphans, and he now stood out with this special label. He was separated in this way from his peers, a gap he bridged by becoming a jokester and making his friends laugh.

5

Gettysburg Academy

IN THE SUMMER OF 1931, sixteen-year-old Tom came from school at Oakham to visit his family in Douglaston. He sailed on the SS *Minnetonka* from London on August 1, 1931 and arrived in New York on August 10, 1931.[1] Tom was morose and dejected upon his arrival because he had an unrequited infatuation with a woman twice his age during the ten-day cross-Atlantic boat trip. He never told his family the reason for his dark mood; instead, he spent the summer avoiding dinners at his grandparents' home and walking aimlessly around New York City.[2] He had little, if any, contact or involvement with John Paul, despite what John Paul might have hoped for; Tom was unavailable and self-absorbed.

Because John Paul is the focus of the current work, there will be no attempt to examine the details of Tom's shipboard infatuation or its effects on his psyche and his mood. Mark Meade includes a description of this romantic event in Tom's life in an article published in the *Merton Journal*, in which he discusses Merton's feelings of turmoil and despair, resulting in suicidal ideation.[3] John Paul and Tom did not speak of the depth of Tom's feelings. John Paul experienced Tom's distance as rejection, without understanding the reasons.

The brothers had last seen each other at the bedside of their dying father. Tom had been present during Owen's last months and at the

1. New York, Passenger and Crew Lists (1931).

2. Merton, T., *Seven Storey Mountain*, 91.

3. Meade, "Thomas Merton's Censored Struggle," 3–15.

funeral service, and John Paul surely had questions about those events that Tom could have answered. Whether he voiced them or not is unknown; whether any answers would have been forthcoming is unlikely. At summer's end on September 12, 1931, Tom returned to England and to his studies at Oakham.[4]

John Paul was enrolled at the Gettysburg Academy in the autumn of 1931; he was twelve years old at the start of the academic year. He wanted to be a scientist.[5] Gettysburg Academy, in Gettysburg, Pennsylvania, was incorporated in 1810 and opened in 1814 as a school for training ministers in the Lutheran faith. When John Paul attended, it was a classic preparatory boarding school for young boys with a curriculum that prepared students for university studies.[6]

There were other suitable schools that were closer to Douglaston; therefore, just how Mattie and Sam decided on Gettysburg Academy is not known. Michael Mott believed Gettysburg Academy was a military school and wrote that John Paul was sent there to learn to follow rules and to behave himself.[7] However, there is no evidence that Gettysburg Academy was ever a military school or that it was ever not affiliated with the Lutheran Chuch.[8] John Paul's first year ended well: he passed all his courses and began to establish a good reputation with the faculty. He returned home at the end of the academic year, looking forward to the summer trip to visit his brother.

The summer trip of 1932 to visit Tom was planned as a two-month stay at the beach resort of Bournemouth on the south coast of England. John Paul and Tom stayed at the Savoy Hotel with their grandparents. Tom was "not surprisingly, the avant-garde teenager with communist leanings, [who] felt rebellious and expressed his rebellion by neglecting his relatives."[9] Tom had been ill in the previous months and was not inclined to be sociable. He had become embroiled in the tangles of another girl's rejection; he sat in the hotel and stared at the English Channel. He was uncommunicative

---

4. Mott, *Seven Mountains of Thomas Merton*, 59.

5. Merton, T., *Road to Joy*, 57.

6. Gettysburg College, "Huber Hall."

7. Mott, *Seven Mountains of Thomas Merton*, 103.

8. "Transformative Places, Resilient Spaces," Gettysburg College, https://www.gettysburg.edu/news/stories?id=dee02b07-33e7-4ce6-985e-eed77423d127.

9. Furlong, *Merton: A Biography*, 55.

during meals and took solitary walks in the Dorset countryside,[10] leaving John Paul to cope with his antisocial and grumpy behavior. For John Paul, it was one more vacation during which Tom remained distant and aloof. John Paul and his grandparents returned to New York from Southampton in August on the SS *Manhattan*.[11]

In 1933, Tom (eighteen years old) booked passage on the SS *Rex* from Genoa, Italy, to New York, arriving March 30, 1933, to visit his family in Douglaston before attending Clare College, Cambridge University.[12] John Paul, who had not yet reached his fifteenth birthday, would have remembered the previous summer in Bournemouth, but he held out hope that he could connect with his big brother. But this summer was no different than the last. The visit began with Tom and Sam having an argument about communism. Dinners were enlivened by debates among Sam, Harold, and Tom about politics, religion, church attendance, sermons, and any other topic that Tom could think of to establish his identity. Tom spent most of his time in Greenwich Village debating about communism with friends, going to Coney Island, or to Jones Beach, all distractions that kept John Paul from seeing his brother.[13]

Tom was to begin Clare College, Cambridge in the fall term. In September, he booked a return passage on the SS *Manhattan* and returned to England, docking at Plymouth on September 19, 1933.[14]

John Paul returned to Gettysburg Academy, where he was associate editor of the 1934 class yearbook, *The Old Spirit of Gettysburg Academy*.[15] As an upper-middle classman he achieved second honors in academics. He was on the rifle team and is shown in a team photo dressed smartly in suit and tie holding his rifle. The yearbook included a humorous exercise in which each one in his class was named and the question posed, "What if…?" For John Paul, now called "Mert" by his mates, the answer was, "What if Wildman Mert wasn't wild!" It goes without saying that the antics he and his brother had gotten into in the Jenkins home were continued at Gettysburg. He was having a good time but avoided going beyond the bounds of acceptable behavior (he didn't risk expulsion). In fact, he was well-liked

---

10. Mott, *Seven Mountains of Thomas Merton*, 63.

11. New York, Passenger and Crew Lists (1932).

12. New York, Passenger and Crew Lists (1933).

13. Mott, *Seven Mountains of Thomas Merton*, 73.

14. New York, Passenger Lists (1933).

15. U.S. School Yearbooks (1880–2012).

by the faculty and students and was considered a good student. He was thought of as a "sweet boy" who was a serious reader and a good writer.[16]

In the summer of 1934, the family did not travel to Europe, instead, Tom came to Douglaston after finishing his first year at Clare College, Cambridge University.[17] Tom had spent the year partying and enjoying the benefits allowed by his trust fund. According to Robert Giroux, Tom fathered an illegitimate child while in Cambridge (Giroux provides no citation for the statement).[18] Tom's guardian, Dr. Tom Bennett, severely reprimanded him for the manner in which the year was spent and told him he ought to remain in the United States of America.[19] Thus, when he left England for Douglaston that summer, he had essentially burned his bridges with the university and his guardian. Sometime during the summer in Douglaston, Tom learned that his scholarship had been withdrawn, eliminating any chance of returning to Clare College. In this way, Tom became a resident in the Jenkinses' home, and thereby thrust into proximity with John Paul, the brother he rejected and from whom he had distanced himself since early childhood.

Tom was not used to being singled out and criticized by his guardian, Dr. Tom Bennett; he had not been chastised in this way before. His response was to respond to rejection with rejection.[20] He was filled with anger at everything, including his family.[21] Tom had asked, and Bennett agreed, that his grandparents not be told why he was dropped from Clare College.[22] While Tom avoided public embarrassment, it is unclear what the family understood of his situation.

Surprisingly, during the summer of 1934, the relationship of the brothers became less contentious. Perhaps the age difference had begun to even out as they both grew and matured. Fifteen-year-old John Paul relished the friendship of his nineteen-year-old brother. John Paul and Tom spent time together listening to music, swimming in Little Neck Bay, and going to movies.[23]

16. Stanley, "Pigeon, Caged, Drowns," 27.

17. New York, Passenger and Crew Lists (1934).

18. Giroux, "Introduction," xii.

19. Mott, *Seven Mountains of Thomas Merton*, 85.

20. Mott, *Seven Mountains of Thomas Merton*, 88.

21. Merton, T., *Run to the Mountain*, 34.

22. Mott, *Seven Mountains of Thomas Merton*, 84.

23. Merton, T., *Seven Storey Mountain*, 148.

Neither Tom nor John Paul had any concern for the proprieties of the Douglaston residents. Both John Paul and Tom were resentful of the local residents for their disparaging remarks about their parents: Ruth was known as a woman who had worn outlandish clothes, had outlandish opinions, and starved herself to the point of death (not a fact), while Owen was known as a man who had been odd, proud, and ineffective—a man who could not provide for the needs of his family.[24] The brothers were known in Douglaston as being badly behaved. There were incidents when they blew up old phonograph records with cherry bombs in the nearby marshes. During a conference at a nearby motel, the brothers used their cherry bombs to blow up a toilet.[25]

As summer ended, John Paul returned to Gettysburg Academy for his last year. Tom returned to England. In order to change his official U.S. government status from a visitor's visa to resident alien status, the law required Tom to leave the United States and make application for more permanent status. There is no record of how Tom spent the time in England. He did not apologize to Tom Bennett for the circumstances that led to his dismissal from Clare College or for the inconvenience and disappointment it caused Bennett.[26] Tom eventually returned to Douglaston in late 1934,[27] residing at the Jenkinses' home, and continuing his education at Columbia University.

There are no school records of the 1934–1935 academic year for Gettysburg Academy. John Paul's class at the Academy was the last to graduate from that institution. The Gettysburg Academy graduating class of May 1935 made front page headlines in the local newspaper, with the names of each of the thirty-two seniors listed.[28] The academy closed, becoming part of Gettysburg College.

When John Paul graduated, he had a strong academic background in Latin, French, American history, ancient history, science, and math. The faculty would later remember him as a boy who had a voracious appetite for reading and was a good writer.[29]

John Paul was well prepared for the next stage of his life. Not yet seventeen years old, he was a sophisticated young man whose grandparents

24. Mott, *Seven Mountains of Thomas Merton*, 252.

25. Mott, *Seven Mountains of Thomas Merton*, 86.

26. Forest, *Living with Wisdom*, 37.

27. New York, Passenger and Crew Lists (1934).

28. "Last Graduation Held by Academy," 1.

29. Stanley, "Pigeon, Caged, Drowns," 27.

had provided him with a classical education. Dinner parties at his home were a regular occurrence, and his neighbors were well-placed business owners and executives. He had sailed across the Atlantic four times and experienced a variety of cultures and countries. He had stayed in the best hotels in London and Paris, and visited chateaux in France, museums in Switzerland, and the countryside in England, including Stratford-upon-Avon. He was academically successful, a good writer, and adept with a rifle. According to Tom, John Paul was generally well balanced, with a quick intelligence, and was sensitive, optimistic, and naturally happy.[30]

From left: Tom, Sam Jenkins, and John Paul in Douglaston. Used with permission of the Merton Legacy Trust and the Thomas Merton Center at Bellarmine University.

30. Merton, T., *Seven Storey Mountain*, 151.

6

Cornell University

Freshman (1935–1936)

THE CAMPUS OF CORNELL University sits on a hill above the south end of
Cayuga Lake, the second largest of the Finger Lakes in Upper New York
State. When students arrive, they are greeted by a spectacular display of autumn color surrounding an idyllic lake. When John Paul arrived in the autumn of 1935, the campus was a beehive of activity. Everyone was anxiously
looking forward to the gridiron game at Schoellkopf Field between Cornell
and St. Lawrence University. John Paul would have paid special attention
to *The Cornell Daily Sun* (the student paper) for information that included
the football team schedule for the season. In addition, the *Sun* carried the
names of men who had pledged fraternities, including John Paul's, for he
pledged the New York Chapter of Sigma Alpha Epsilon. He is pictured in a
group photograph in the 1936 yearbook, seated in the bottom row looking
rather glum.[1] He flirted with membership in the fraternity, but eventually
rejected fraternity life. He and three friends rented a house in town that
they dubbed "The Grand Hotel."[2]

John Paul was an average student at a university that required above-
average performance. When compared to his classmates on a scholastic ap-
titude test (Ohio State Psychological Test) his score placed him in the tenth

1. U.S. School Yearbooks (1900–1990), *Cornellian.* 229.
2. Merton, T., *Seven Storey Mountain*, 151.

percentile.[3] To succeed he would have to work very hard and be extremely disciplined. His college career becomes somewhat transparent only with the benefit of his transcript. Reading between the lines enables the reader to discern what John Paul was like as a college student. To say only that he got bad grades would be accurate but incomplete; a look at the details of both his course selection and his grades provides insight into the difficulties that afflicted his academic career at Cornell and later in the Royal Canadian Air Force. His experience at Cornell was marred by both a lack of coherent and consistence guidance from an engaged and concerned faculty member or a parent, and by his own lack of discipline.

As a first-year student in the fall of 1935, John Paul still wanted to be a scientist, accordingly, he registered for six courses: Chemistry 101, Chemistry 102, English 3, Mathematics 1, French 3, Hygiene 1, and a non-credit course called Drill. He failed one chemistry course and passed the other courses with a grade less than or equal to 75 percent. During the school year, he wrote letters to his family showing his lack of a defined goal, causing his grandparents and Tom concern.[4] In the second semester of his first year (Spring 1936), he was placed on probation, and he passed chemistry, English, math, hygiene, French, and drill with minimally acceptable grades. At the end of his first year, he went home to Douglaston tired and disgusted and kept all of this to himself. He was not one to speak about his troubles and did not want to cause distress to others. He was not pleased with his grades and promised himself he would do better the next year. To make up for his first semester "F" in chemistry, he took a chemistry course at Columbia during the summer of 1936 and passed with a grade of "C"; however, he waited until December 1938 (nearly two and a half years later) to petition Cornell to accept the credits for the course, a petition the school denied.

Sophomore (1936–1937)

In his sophomore year, 1936 to 1937, he repeated the same pattern of course selection that he had in his first year, registering for Chemistry 205, Chemistry 206, Physics 7, History 21 (a medieval history course), German 1, and Drill in the autumn. Adding physics to an already difficult course load

3. Merton, J. P. Cornell Transcript, 1935–1940. The transcript was obtained by the author through the Cornell Registrar's Office; all details about courses John Paul took at Cornell and the status of them (pass/fail) are from his Cornell transcript (1935–1940).

4. Merton, T., *Seven Storey Mountain*, 151.

when he was on probation is curious. The fall semester was abruptly interrupted in October, when his grandfather Sam died in his sleep.[5] John Paul went home for the funeral at the Fresh Pond Crematory where his mother was cremated (he had not been allowed to attend her funeral). Sam's death had a devastating effect on him, as Sam was the only father figure he knew; he failed all course work that semester.

In the spring of 1937, John Paul registered for courses including German, history, public speaking, psychology, and French. In February, he was placed on probation, and in April, his probationary period was continued with a warning. For the entire academic year, he failed, dropped, or took a grade of incomplete in all but his psychology course, which he passed with 72 percent.

John Paul returned to Douglaston in May of 1937 to begin what was to be a summer of emotional upheaval in his life. In July, Cornell informed John Paul that he had been dropped and would not be able to return to school in the fall. He abandoned his dream to be a scientist. Overall, he spoke little about college or his plight. He went to the wedding of his boyhood friend Russ Boyers. John Paul had no girlfriend to accompany him, so he went to the wedding with his brother.[6]

In June, Tom moved out of the Jenkinses' home to rent an apartment on 114th Street in Manhattan. In August, Mattie Jenkins died.[7] She, too, was cremated in Fresh Pond Crematory, where, again, the memory of the loss of his mother complicated his grief over the loss of both grandparents. With Mattie's death and Tom's move, John Paul lost, except for his Uncle Harold, his entire family. Harold and John Paul continued to live in the house on Virginia Avenue, but the absence of Mattie, the heart of the home, left a hole that could not be filled.

That summer of 1937 was a challenge for John Paul. Harold was courting and would eventually marry Elsie Hauck Holahan. With Harold preoccupied by his relationship to Elsie, John Paul was virtually alone, without the support, attachment, and love he yearned for. Both grandparents had died; Tom had moved out of the family home in Douglaston. At eighteen years of age, John Paul was unable to return to Cornell, the locus of his friends, so he worked as a laborer for the Coldwell Wingate Co. from June until October of 1937. He was laid off in October and then worked briefly

5. Forest, *Living with Wisdom*, 48.

6. Merton, T., *Run to the Mountain*, 370.

7. New York City Health Department, Death Certificates (1937).

for a metal construction company and then as a clerk at Hearn Co. from November 1937 through January 1938. [8]

1938: Probation

John Paul prevailed upon Cornell to cancel his status of "Dropped," although the rationale he used is not known. Given his record, he must have been very persuasive, charming, and solicitous for Cornell to grant his request. Cornell accepted him for the spring semester 1938; however, while rescinding his dismissal, the record noted that he was to return on probationary status (his third probation) and would be carefully monitored (the details of the monitoring plan were not stated). With this plan, he returned to Cornell for the spring semester (his third year). Notably, John Paul, having given up his dream to be a scientist, elected only liberal arts courses for the spring of 1938: a psychology course, two French classes, economics, and a philosophy course. He passed all his courses and ended his third year with success. The difference between the semesters in which he failed and the spring semester of 1938 in which he passed appears to be both the careful monitoring of his work, as specified in the readmission notes in his transcript, and the types of courses taken (liberal arts instead of science).

1938–39: Academic Monitoring

He began the fall semester of 1938 with the benefit of close monitoring. Although he was permitted to enroll in eighteen credit hours, given his prior performance, the wisdom of this decision appears questionable, especially as eighteen credit hours in a semester would have required special approval, according to the school guidelines. How he was able to obtain the special approval is unknown. In the fall semester, he took three economics courses, English, and two history courses. He passed all but one of the economics courses: he failed to attend the final examination. In the spring of 1939, he took three history courses: French, German, and a course called "Government" (possibly political science). He passed the history courses (completing two of them late: one in July and the other in September) and German but failed French and Government.

---

8. Ottawa, Canada, Library and Archives, "WWII Service Files of War Dead (1939–1947)." (John Paul's work history is detailed in his service file.)

In the summer of 1939, he met Leonard Miscall when he was attracted to the Russian wolfhound Len was walking.[9] When he spoke to Len, it was mutual admiration from the start. Len was a forty-one-year-old consulting engineer with his own business. His wife, Rovene (nee Whitaker), was a social worker with the Works Progress Administration. Their sixteen-year-old daughter Marilynn was a high school student and their seven-year-old son Jack was in grade school.[10]

John Paul was welcomed into the Miscall home and soon became such a frequent visitor that he was considered family. Certainly, John Paul was an affable young man who seemed to get along with everyone, but what developed into deep ties to the Miscall family so soon after the loss of Sam and Mattie appears providential. No record exists to describe what Len Miscall saw in John Paul that prompted him to invite a college student he met casually on the street to his home, but there, John Paul became a member of a family,[11] and even more importantly, he became what he had always longed for: a big brother (to Len's daughter Marilynn and son Jack). He spent considerable time with Marilynn because of her interest in the arts and his expertise in photography. John Paul showed her how to use his Leica camera and to take pictures during the hikes they took in the nearby woodlands, and yet, John Paul never wavered from his chosen role as a "brother." He continued to relate to Marilynn as to a sister, and no romance developed between them.[12]

What John Paul enjoyed most about the Miscalls was conversation about topics in which he could make his point of view without strong reactions.[13] He had memories of Sam Jenkins discussing his viewpoints with little tolerance for disagreement. With the Miscalls, the discussions of politics, the impending war, social justice issues, and wolfhounds were stimulating. These kinds of conversations had not happened with his brother. Although Tom needed to talk things out in conversation in order to find his own mind,[14] he did not engage John Paul, while Len and Rovene did. The Miscalls tolerated no hijinks, and John Paul was only too keen to be

9. Stanley, "Pigeon, Caged, Drowns," 34.

10. U.S. Federal Census (1940).

11. Mott, *Seven Mountains of Thomas Merton*, 116.

12. Stanley, "Pigeon, Caged, Drowns," 34.

13. Stanley, "Pigeon, Caged, Drowns," 39.

14. Mott, *Seven Mountains of Thomas Merton*, 123.

accepted. Their influence was so keen that John Paul eventually bought his own wolfhound.[15]

1939–40: Dismissal

The 1939–1940 academic year began with news that Germany had invaded Poland (September 1, 1939). On September 3, 1939, Great Britain and France declared war on Germany. The United States remained neutral, sending armaments and ships but no troops. War was on every person's mind in the United States, a hotly debated topic: should the United States remain neutral or go to war with Germany? Len Miscall, while a student at Cornell during WWI, had enlisted and served in the Student Army Training Corps.[16] While not urging enlistment to John Paul, he supported active engagement by the United States. As John Paul spent much time in the Miscall home, he was heavily influenced by Len's opinions,[17] especially since Len modeled the father for which he longed.

John Paul began his fifth year at Cornell in the fall of 1939, taking four history courses and a fine arts course and passed all but one history course, failing again to take the final examination. In the spring of 1940, John Paul had a course load that calls into doubt his continued "close monitoring," taking three history courses, Greek, Latin, and Russian, and a fine arts course, which seems an unmanageable course load for someone with a record of academic failure. The record notes that a Professor Stephenson granted John Paul permission to enroll in at least one history course that required a prerequisite John Paul did not have. In the end, he passed only that history course and the Russian language class. He failed to attend the final examinations for Latin and Greek.

At the end of spring term 1940, John Paul had been at Cornell for five years, had completed nine semesters, been on probation three times, and had ninety-nine of the 120 credits needed for a degree. He did not graduate; his transcript shows there was an "honorable dismissal as to character only," issued in June 1940. His character or personal conduct were not the issue. He had spent five years at Cornell following a trajectory that had no clear destination, but he had broken no rules and had committed no infractions for which he had been disciplined. This time, he was dropped from

15. Stanley, "Pigeon, Caged, Drowns," 39.

16. New York, "Abstracts of WWI Military Service (1917–1919)."

17. Stanley, "Pigeon, Caged, Drowns," 34.

enrollment permanently. Tom visited Ithaca for a few days in June 1940, presumably anticipating a graduation celebration. Tom learned from John Paul that he would not graduate but either never discussed the reasons for the failure or chose not to describe them in his autobiography.

The issue was, in part, his failure to consistently apply himself to his studies. A confounding factor was his age (he was sixteen when he arrived at Cornell to begin his freshman year), and the fact that he had virtually no guidance from any mentor. Although Sam and Mattie were loving, they were also elderly. Shepherding a young man to full adulthood was a task for which they had no energy. John Paul was left to find his way through adolescence and into adulthood on his own.

John Paul was indeed a charming young man and a good conversationalist; he was confident and probably unreasonably optimistic about his own capabilities. Tom's friends found John Paul to be pleasant and charming.[18] Ed Rice, a close friend of Tom, said, "when I knew him, in 1940 and 1941, he was a wild blond kid, tremendously likable and probably further out than any of us."[19]

These characteristics probably accounted for his success in persuading Cornell to rescind his dismissal in 1938. This is also what enabled him to persuade two professors to admit him to their advanced classes without having taken the prerequisite courses.

It was only his determination and self-confidence that allowed him to persist in the face of poor grades. He did not have the study or organizational skills needed for success. With academic monitoring, his grades improved, but his was not the style to accept continual help.

His course selection was a patchwork quilt of subjects without any sustained emphasis on a major area of concentration. Science courses were emphasized in his first two years. After the debacle of those semesters, his interest seemed to turn toward history or economics. Languages were the only consistent thread in his course selection, yet he had to repeat courses for French. It is striking that in his last term he took Greek, Latin, and Russian language courses. There seems no logical reason for this selection, and it must be assumed he was simply just interested in them at the time, without any sense of how they fit into his need to graduate.

In addition to his pattern of poor grades, one additional factor must be considered. In November 1939, John Paul turned twenty-one years old.

18. Mott, *Seven Mountains of Thomas Merton*, 152.

19. Rice, *Man in the Sycamore Tree*, 63.

The significance of this concerns the trust funds that his grandfather established and on which he was living. Following Sam's death in 1937, John Paul's Uncle Harold had been appointed his guardian and managed the funds until John Paul turned twenty-one. With his twenty-first birthday, he was financially on his own, free to spend money as he wished. He did just that, purchasing cameras, cars, fancy razors, fishing tackle, microscopes, movie cameras, radios, and rifles.[20]

He began the spring semester of 1940 with the benefit of several trust funds that Sam had set up. These would have given him an annual income of more than enough for him to support himself, trust funds that made him a rich man.[21] John Paul attended Cornell during the Great Depression, and yet, he spent the spring semester of 1940 taking flying lessons at the local airport in Ithaca. Flying lessons were a luxury, and, for most Depression era households, completely out of reach financially.

During the summer of 1940, not only was John Paul's world falling apart with the loss of family and a failed bachelor's degree, but the world at large was in chaos. The war in Europe was intensifying. The Maginot Line had not held, and Hitler's armies had run through France. The British army was pushed to the westernmost coast of France at Dunkirk, with their backs to the English Channel. The Battle of Dunkirk began in May 1940 and lasted until early June. Trapped on the coast, thousands of British soldiers were massacred, although 114,000 lives were rescued by a flotilla of small boats of every type that crossed the Channel from England. These ordinary citizens responded to a call for help from the military. They took as many aboard as they could hold and brought them to safety back across the Channel.

In July 1940, the Battle of Britain began and lasted until October of the same year. The British Royal Air Force was at war with the German Luftwaffe. This battle was crucial since it was meant to demoralize and damage the English in advance of a full-scale invasion by the German army. The German Luftwaffe began the Blitz of London in September 1940 with fifty-seven days of consecutive night bombing. The Blitz lasted nine months, until May 1941. Due to the heroic efforts of many young pilots, Great Britain defeated the Luftwaffe in the Battle of Britain, and Hitler abandoned his plans for invasion. [22]

20. Mott, *Seven Mountains of Thomas Merton*, 103.

21. Stanley, "Pigeon, Caged, Drowns," 32.

22. "Blitz: The Hardest Night."

In September 1940, the American Congress passed the Selective Training and Service Act. It was the first peacetime conscription in United States history and was not a surprise to John Paul. He could see that American neutrality would be short-lived. He anticipated America's entry into the war in Europe and knew the United States Congress was discussing the draft. He did not mind serving in the military but did not want to be in the infantry, which meant he wanted to avoid the draft, not the war.

That summer of 1940, he made two attempts to enlist in the American armed forces. He drove to New York City, and at the Church Street recruitment center, signed up for a United States Navy program that would result in a commission following successful completion of a two-week cruise in the West Indies. He was a candidate on the cruise, but it did not turn out as he hoped. He and the commanding officer had some unspecified disagreement, and he was not selected. He also tried to enlist in the United States Army. In an interview with Michael Mott, Pat Holahan Priest, who was a girlfriend of John Paul during their teenage years, told Mott that John Paul had tried to join the Army but failed the psychological test. [23]

In *The Seven Storey Mountain*, Tom states that John Paul visited him in the autumn of 1940 in Olean, New York, where Tom was teaching at St. Bonaventure College.[24] However, a visitor's card dated September 2, 1940, issued in Tapachula, Mexico (the capital city of the state of Chiapas), near the border with Guatemala and the Pacific Ocean, shows John Paul in Mexico.[25] Given driving time from New York to Mexico, John Paul probably left New York sometime in August; the visit to Tom in Olean probably actually occurred during the summer months.

During his visit to Olean, John Paul and Tom spoke of the coming draft and John Paul's lack of success in joining the Army or the Navy. Tom did not want John Paul to enlist and was pleased with his failed attempts. John Paul told his brother that if he could not get into the military, he would go to Mexico to take pictures of Mayan temples.[26] Ed Rice, a friend of Tom's, had asked John Paul what he would do if he couldn't get into the

---

23. Mott, *Seven Mountains of Thomas Merton*, 158.

24. Merton, T., *Seven Storey Mountain*, 309.

25. Ottawa, Canada, Library and Archives, "WWII Service Files of War Dead (1939–1947)."

26. Merton, T., *Seven Storey Mountain*, 309.

military, and John Paul is quoted as saying, "Oh, drive around Mexico until I run out of gas."[27]

Journey to Mexico

What was this journey about? Life had not gone well at Cornell. He had no university degree and no job prospects. By July 1940, John Paul had left "home" for good.[28] Douglaston was a place of the past, no longer home. His brother had moved out of the family home and his Uncle Harold was preoccupied with his relationship to Elsie. John Paul had no love interest. His trip to Mexico was impetuous and without purpose or direction. Perhaps he simply removed himself from any further devastating losses of attachment.

John Paul was in Mexico for nine months; he learned some of the language, saw the Mayan ruins, and met with many of the locals. The Mayan ruins of the Aztecs in Tapachula date back to the thirteenth century. John Paul photographed the most famous of them, Chichen Itza and Uxmal; he may well have stopped to see ruins in Sayil, Labina, and Kabah. During the trip there was some excitement when he drove in the area of Colima that suffered a 7.6 magnitude earthquake in April 1941, killing ninety people.[29]

For a time, John Paul stayed with an American rancher in Saint Luis Potosi, Central Mexico.[30] The rancher told him of his financial problems. Because of John Paul's good-natured empathy for others, he loaned the man $3,500 with the understanding that the loan would be repaid. Their agreement was that if the money was not repaid, John Paul would own part of the ranch. There exist no records of this transaction. Based on what is known of John Paul's easy-going approach to life and his belief in the essential goodness of others, it can be assumed this transaction was based only on a verbal promise and a handshake. There is no record of either the money being repaid or of John Paul taking ownership of a portion of a ranch in Mexico.

After John Paul's return from Mexico in May 1941, he visited his brother in Olean, New York, at St. Bonaventure College where Tom was teaching.[31]

27. Rice, *Man in the Sycamore Tree*, 63.

28. Mott, *Seven Mountains of Thomas Merton*, 159.

29. Merton, T., *Run to the Mountain*, 360.

30. Merton, T., *Seven Storey Mountain*, 335.

31. Merton, T., *Seven Storey Mountain*, 335.

Tom at St. Bonaventure College. Photo taken by John Paul Merton. Used with permission of the Merton Legacy Trust and the Thomas Merton Center at Bellarmine University.

John Paul shared his adventures. The back seat of his Buick was filled with souvenirs, including Mexican records, pictures, a revolver, a machete, and colored baskets, among other things. He and Tom talked about the pending entry of America into the war, and they hacked weeds with his new machete.[32] One can only imagine what Tom thought of John Paul's stories of shooting a snake with his newly acquired pistol, narrowly missing an earthquake near Mexico City, or loaning money to the rancher.

Tom did not approve of taking pictures of blood-soaked stones that were once the libation of gods of forgotten generations of Mayans.[33] John Paul may have sensed his brother's disapproval as he was sharing the thrills of the trip.

John Paul went back to Ithaca, to the comfort of the Miscall household.[34] The Miscalls greeted his return with genuine enthusiasm. He spent the summer relaxing with the Miscall family, pondering what to do next and generally letting life take its course. Although he lived two streets away from the Miscall address, he was almost a permanent resident of their home. They thought of him as family, and he loved them as family. He also spent time with his friends in town, talking about the war, the draft, and

32. Mott, *Seven Mountains of Thomas Merton*, 180.

33. Merton, T., *Seven Storey Mountain*, 309.

34. Stanley, "Pigeon, Caged, Drowns," 42.

whether they should wait for the United States to enter the war, or join the RCAF. They were eager to get into the action.

Going off to war was not something he took lightly, but he was not going to wait for the war to come to him. He dreamed of doing something that would give his life greater meaning. He had spent the last years in an aimless pursuit of whatever came next but had no idea which way the path would take him. This war had the effect of giving him a focus that had been lacking. It helped him realize the things that mattered in his life. He had tried unsuccessfully to enlist in the United States Armed Forces. As sentiment in the country was not favorable for sending troops to fight in a foreign war, he had no hope that he could get into the thick of the fight as a member of the United States military. For this reason, he and his like-minded friends began to investigate a way to enter the military in some other country. The closest opportunity lay in Canada.

7

Royal Canadian Air Force

WAR CHANGES MORE THAN borders and boundaries of nations. War changes lives. World War II changed millions of lives. The worldwide death total is estimated at 15 million battle deaths and 45 million civilian deaths. The United Kingdom suffered 450,700 military and civilian deaths, and the United States 416,800 deaths.[1] Of the 120,000 men and women who served in British Bomber Command, 55,573 lives were lost.[2]

This story focuses on just one airman.[3] The war both transformed John Paul and precipitated his desire for a greater spirituality, manifested through his baptism into Catholicism. His unstructured lifestyle was transformed by the military discipline of the RCAF. The law of love he lived with a humanist worldview was transformed into a spiritual ethos with his change of religious denomination from Episcopalian to Catholicism; however, the new version of himself happened gradually as do most transformations.

How his idea to join the Canadian fighting forces came about is unclear. He had English relatives living in Surrey and must have known of his New Zealand family and their military service, so it seems the natural fit for him would have been the British Royal Air Force. On the other hand, he may have simply taken the path of least resistance: Canada was close and

---

1. National WWII Museum, "Worldwide Deaths in World War II."

2. See the Canadian Royal Air Force Bomber Command Museum at https://www. bombercommandmuseum.ca.

3. Canada, Ottawa, Library and Archives, "WWII Service Files of War Dead (1939–1947)."

already involved in the war effort. On September 3, 1939, the British Parliament passed the National Service Act, which began the conscription of Great Britain's men into the military. John Paul was not subject to this conscription but welcomed the opportunity to enlist. The recruitment office in Toronto was approximately 250 miles from Ithaca. He probably was influenced by his friends, with whom he hatched the plan. One of John Paul's acquaintances, David Fairbanks, went on to become an ace pilot in the RCAF.

Prior to enlisting in the RCAF, John Paul may have been aware of his maternal grandmother's Quaker background and his mother's pacifist conviction during WWI, his father's conscientious objector status in WWI, and his brother's refusal to kill in war.[4] Had Ruth been alive, she would have strongly urged against his enlisting, while Owen may have been ambivalent. Tom is known to have tried to convince John Paul not to enlist and asked the Miscalls to do the same.[5] It seemed John Paul was the only member of his family who was *not* a conscientious objector.

The focus of his mother's life was family, writing, and interior design, for Owen, it was painting, and for Tom, writing. John Paul's focus was to be present to and for other people. He tried to do the right thing as he reached out to others. After all, he had spent years of his childhood summers reaching out to his father and brother for a connection. Tom thought John Paul had not assessed the dangers of war realistically and assumed that for John Paul it was as easy to fly a bomber as it was to drive his Buick.[6] But Tom, who never really knew his younger brother, did not understand what motivated John Paul.

First, John Paul desired relationship—the very human connection that had been denied him by his brother and father—and he sought a purpose that would enable him to minister to others, to care for them, a way of fulfilling his own longing for a caring parent. John Paul had to have recognized that military service would bring him the connection he sought with a camaraderie of men devoted to the same cause. Further, he saw the war effort as a way of caring for those oppressed.

The world was at war, and he was not going to sit by and avoid it. He was going to show up and be part of the action. Whatever the course, he was not going to wait for his letter from the draft board. He would not

4. Merton, T., *Seven Storey Mountain*, 312.

5. Stanley, "Pigeon, Caged, Drowns," 41.

6. Merton, T., *Seven Storey Mountain*, 355.

be drafted; it was not his way. Despite his brother's advice to the contrary, he volunteered.

There were several efforts to assist Americans who wanted to volunteer for the war effort, one of them arranged by Charles Sweeney, an American. Sweeney's nephew, of the same name, worked in London. Both were helping to recruit volunteers for the British Royal Air Force. In the United States, the elder Sweeney recruited about thirty men to be pilots and paid for their transport to Canada and then to Britain. In London, the younger Sweeney recruited Americans living in London who wanted to be pilots for the Home Guard. These units were approved by the British Air Ministry in July 1940 and became known as Eagle Squadrons.[7] Three Eagle Squadrons were formed between September 1940 and July 1941. These squadrons flew as units of the Royal Air Force under Fighter Command. The requirements to join an Eagle Squadron included a high school diploma, age between twenty and thirty-one years, good eyesight, and 300 hours of certified flying time.[8]

The debate continued both in the United States Congress and in the country as a whole regarding entry into the war. The United States first decided to maintain neutrality in the face of increasing hostility in Europe, and between 1935 and 1939, three Neutrality Acts were passed by the United States Congress. The Acts prohibited the export of "arms, ammunition, and implements of war" from the United States to foreign nations at war and required arms manufacturers in the United States to apply for an export license.[9]

The British armed forces required all members to swear an oath of allegiance to the Crown. This oath of allegiance was waived for foreign nationals in June 1940, when the Canadian government passed an Order in Council. The oath of allegiance was replaced with an oath of obedience, requiring only obedience to the rules and discipline of the RCAF. The British needed pilots badly. So now the way was clear. As of December 1941, there were 6,129 American members of the RCAF.[10]

Whatever John Paul's motive, on August 25, 1941, he drove to Toronto and took his physical examination as the first step in enlisting in the RCAF. He was two months shy of his twenty-third birthday. The report showed

7. American Battle Monuments Commission, "Eagle Squadrons of WWII."
8. Caine, *Eagles of the RAF*, loc. 785; Mehuron, "Eagle Squadrons."
9. U.S. State Department, "Neutrality Acts, 1930s."
10. Halliday, "Canada's Yanks."

he was in excellent health, although the examiner noted he was tense, off-balance, and somewhat nervous. He stood five feet eleven inches, was broad shouldered, had blue eyes and blond hair and a fair complexion. He listed his occupation as "photographer." When asked to state what special qualifications he had that would be useful to the service, he listed photography, driving, swimming skills, hunting ability, and a speaking knowledge of Spanish. In his typical humorous style, he listed English as a language skill.[11]

Three days later he completed an Attestation Form (Application Form) and was interviewed by Flight Officer Key in the Toronto recruitment office. In the interview report, Key described John Paul as a clean-cut chap with a good education who "should readily absorb training." He was confident, clear spoken, and sincere. Key judged him to be suitable for the commissioned ranks, fitted for the role of pilot. Of the three roles for aircrew at the time—pilot, observer, or air gunner— John Paul had chosen pilot. At enlistment he had only eight hours of dual flight control at the Ithaca airport where he took lessons; however, he clearly hoped he would be trained as a pilot in the RCAF.

John Paul had made a fine impression in this interview; for all he knew, he was headed to be an RCAF pilot. He was off to begin training in Canada and then to the war in England. The enlistment papers record the date of enlistment as September 8, 1941. After his enlistment, he gave up his apartment and stayed with the Miscalls whenever he had a weekend pass.[12] He relaxed with his adopted family and took hikes with Marilynn, continuing her photography lessons.

Whatever he was thinking at the time, it quickly became clear to him that his life had changed dramatically. A few weeks prior, he had been a carefree, well-traveled, and educated young man who had enough money to do whatever he chose. He was affable and enjoyed a group of like-minded friends. He was easily met, well-spoken, and a good conversationalist. Without much direction in his life or attention to the details of everyday life, he had managed by seeking out as many experiences as he could. He lived in the moment, harmed no one, and sought the acquaintance of many. He needed discipline in college but did not have it. He now faced the challenge of military discipline but was not deterred; instead, he was optimistic that he would become a pilot.

11. Ottawa, Canada, Library and Archives, "WWII Service Files of War Dead (1939–1947)."

12. Stanley, "Pigeon, Caged, Drowns," 49.

Training, detailed in his service record, took most of the next year. John Paul was sent first to Trenton, Canada, for several months of initial training, and then to Western Canada for aircrew training. The instructors not only graded each student's performance, but also commented on each student's attitude and style of functioning. These remarks give some insight into the kind of person John Paul was at this period of his life and shed light on the issues that had kept him from success at Cornell, for the RCAF instructors were very clear in their descriptions of the manner in which he performed the classroom work. It is, therefore, enlightening to cite them here.

John Paul had just turned twenty-three years old when he began training. He was among the thousands of men and women who served and took on responsibilities beyond anything they had previously known. Despite all of John Paul's college experience, he never appeared to have a mentor who provided direction and guidance to help him transition into full adulthood. Neither did he receive this type of support from his family. By all accounts, until he enlisted in the RCAF, he was navigating life on his own. The discipline of military life must have posed a huge challenge for him, and yet, it did not deter him.

As John Paul progressed through Initial Training School from November 10, 1941 to January 2, 1942 in Trenton, Canada, he soon faced a disciplined, structured lifestyle. Trenton was the largest training center for the British Commonwealth Air Training Program during the war. Instructors expected John Paul to master the theory of flight, meteorology, navigation, duties of an air officer, military administration, algebra, and trigonometry. At the conclusion of this training, he ranked forty-six in a class of 127 pupils. His instructors remarked that he was a good lad with a good background, who seriously wanted to fly, spoke Spanish and a bit of Russian but noted that he needed a lot of help and could be temperamental. While at Trenton, the Japanese bombed Pearl Harbor on December 7, 1941, and the United States declared war with Germany on December 11, 1941. Had John Paul waited a bit more than three months he would have been able to join the U.S. Army Air Corps.

At the end of this training sequence, candidates were posted to either pilot training or air observer training. Despite the recommendation of the recruiting officer in Toronto, John Paul had not qualified for training as a pilot. He was to become an air observer.

The air observer designation for a bomber crew was one with several duties at the beginning of the war. The air observer was the navigator and bomb aimer, responsible for guiding the plane to its target and making the decision to release the bombs. There was a place in the fuselage for a navigator's chart table where he worked until the plane was close to its target. At that point he would change position and move to the nose of the plane. As bomb aimer, the air observer directed the pilot in the approach to the target. Lying flat in the nose of the plane, the air observer directed the pilot until the bombs were released, and then took a photograph to show bombs had been released.

The geodesic frame of the Wellington bomber. The Bomb Aimer lay prone on the floor in the nose of the plane to the side of the pilot. Used with permission of Brooklands Museum Trust Ltd, Surrey, United Kingdom.

The sequence of training in the RCAF at the beginning of World War II was for twelve weeks at an initial training school, then to advanced observer training for a twelve-week course in aerial photography, navigation, and reconnaissance, then to bombing and gunnery school for ten weeks, followed by air navigation school for advanced air observer training for six weeks.[13]

Air observer school at Edmonton in Alberta, Canada lasted from January 5, 1942 to April 11, 1942. This phase had several levels involving aerial photography, navigation, bomb aiming, and reconnaissance. The

13. Commonwealth Air Training Museum, "RCAF Sequence of Training Chart."

navigation techniques included "dead reckoning" and "visual plotting." The air training portion taught both navigation and bomb aiming, while the ground training portion involved the use of maps, plotting, meteorology, use of a compass and instruments, and proper signaling.

Air observer school training was difficult for the best of men but for John Paul, whose talents did not lie in mathematics or science, it was particularly problematic. He worried about his marks and worked hard. He was frustrated with the material and became irritated with some instructors. In a letter from John Paul to his friend Tom O'Brien dated February 2, 1942, he complained that one navigation instructor taught bad technique, and the corporal who taught aerial photography used a defective camera. Use of defective photography equipment was something that John Paul, an expert photographer, found dismaying.

The Japanese bombing of Pearl Harbor three months after John Paul's enlistment caused the United States to enter the war. Surely John Paul felt some disappointment and discouragement that he could have been serving with his own country's armed forces had he waited to enlist. He knew that negotiations were underway to transfer Americans from British to American service, but such an arrangement never materialized for him.

United States enlistees in British armed forces were to be given the opportunity to apply for transfer to American units from April 6 to April 20, 1942. Once having applied, applicants were to be interviewed in Canada by officers from the United States who had power to appoint or enlist them. Similar Canadian boards would discharge or release the personnel. A Canadian-American military board, headed by Major General Guy V. Henry, who was later to become Senior U.S. Army Member of the Permanent Joint Board on Defense, visited thirty-three Canadian cities between May 5 and June 3, 1942. The board eventually transferred approximately 3,000 of the 8,864 American citizens who enlisted in the Canadian Royal Air Force.[14]

An undated letter from John Paul to his friend Tom O'Brian shows his frustration:

> I am getting a little fed up with the idea of all this training which
> may lead to nothing more than a navigator's seat with the coastal
> patrol, a grim business. The prospect of going overseas even in
> August seems pretty nonexistent. As a result I am applying for
> enlistment with both the U.S. Army Air Corps and the Army Air

14. Halliday, "Canada's Yanks."

Corps. If I am going to train or do some stinking routine job I would rather do it on home soil.

John Paul knew of the possibility to transfer his enlistment from the RCAF to the U.S. Army Air Corps, but for some unknown reason he did not transfer. He may not have met the deadline; he may have decided not to take advantage of that option due to a sense of kinship with his mates, or for other reasons.

John Paul managed to just barely pass air observer school training. His rank in class was 26 in a class of 27. His instructors commented that he had needed special attention with only average results. He was noted to be easily discouraged and he had to be monitored closely. He was not recommended for the commissioned ranks or for a position as an instructor. His next stop was Armament Training, which took him to Lethbridge, Alberta, Canada. Armament training consisted of bombing and gunnery school, lasting from April 13 to May 23, 1942.

John Paul was familiar with weapons and had enjoyed the rifle club in high school; he had hunted while at Gettysburg Academy. This training took him to a whole new level. The RCAF weapons training was difficult, but he took to learning the task. Bombing and Air Gunnery exercises taught the techniques of bomb aiming and aerial machine gunnery; training was designed to teach the technique and accuracy of bombing raids. John Paul's instructor commented that he turned in good, high-level work despite the fact that he ranked thirteenth in a class of twenty-eight and that he achieved only 66 percent of accurate bomb drops.

He was qualified to graduate, and on May 23, 1942, he was appointed as an air observer and promoted to the rank of sergeant. On his tunic, he now wore the air observer's single-winged brevet, with a wreath surrounding the letter "O" above the left breast pocket.

John Paul Merton receiving his air observer brevet on his graduation from initial training. He was promoted to the rank of sergeant the same day. Used with permission of the Merton Legacy Trust and the Thomas Merton Center at Bellarmine University.

Before the end of this training, there was a special leave granted from May 24 until June 7, 1942 (no details exist about this leave).

The final step in the air observer sequence of training included advanced air observer training in navigation. For John Paul, navigation training lasted from June 8 to July 20, 1942. It was here that the instructors commented on his overall performance and described his weaknesses. He was described as an excellent young man, with a good education, and he was serious and worked hard, but got only mediocre results. He was slow in absorbing new work, not good at mathematics, not used to detailed work, and better at practical work than classroom work. He was conscientious but was easily discouraged by his own failures. He ranked 210 in a class of 224.

These instructors could have been writing about John Paul while he was at Cornell University. Their remarks capture his approach, his skills, and most of all, his limitations. He struggled with detail and consistency during college, and it was to be the same in the military. Yet, the persistent monitoring and close supervision helped him reach an adequate level of performance to finish training.

John Paul finished his training in Canada in July 1942. He was scheduled to ship out to England for further operational training before becoming a crew member of a bomber, but he had a two-week pre-embarkation leave, which he spent getting his affairs in order and saying goodbye to those he loved. John Paul must have been aware of his chances for survival. In 1942, the life expectancy of crew members of Allied bombers was two weeks. Prior to his departure for England, he made out his will, carefully leaving meaningful items to the people he loved. He had already suffered the loss of his mother, father, and grandparents; he was no stranger to death. For his two-week leave, he planned to visit his uncle Harold in Bethesda, Maryland, then travel to Kentucky, to the Cistercian monastery of the Abbey of Gethsemani near Bardstown, to visit his brother Tom, who had entered the community on December 13, 1941, and then return to Ithaca to spend time with the Miscalls. He was planning to cherish the time with the people he loved.

8

Transformation

In order to understand the totality of John Paul's life in the context of his search for, and ultimately his finding, a spiritual home in Catholicism, it is necessary to correct the impression that his life had been one devoid of grace.

Although Thomas Merton suggests in his narrative of John Paul's visit to Gethsemani (*Seven Storey Mountain*) that his younger brother came to the monastery to be baptized and presents himself as the agent who facilitates his brother becoming Catholic, there are good reasons to believe that John Paul may have already been actively seeking a spiritual home long before that visit. Further, there are reasons to believe that John Paul's attraction to Catholicism, the character of his faith, and the reasons for his actions immediately prior to his death resulted from a lifelong developing spirituality that had little to do with his older brother.

According to Tom, up until the time when John Paul visited Gethsemani in July 1942, John Paul's life was aimless and unhappy because he lacked grace.[1] However, in order to understand Tom's opinion, it is important to understand the moment when the Gethsemani visit occurred, and the mindset of Tom Merton, by whom the only account of this visit is told.

Thomas Merton was writing *Seven Storey Mountain* sometime in 1944; the manuscript was mailed to his literary agent in October 1946. In the early 1940s, Tom was flush with the grace and enthusiasm of his baptism into Catholicism and his vocation into a pre-Vatican II Church. The church

---

1. Merton, T., *Seven Storey Mountain*, 397.

of 1942 was not the Roman Catholic Church of today. Opinionated and dogmatic, the Catholic Church provided answers for all theological and religious questions, never doubting itself. The faithful rested comfortably in the knowledge that the Catholic Church's teachings provided them assurance of right and wrong in an ever-changing world. Mostly, the Catholic Church saw itself as a moral authority; other religious faiths were viewed as "less than," or worse, as *wrong*.[2]

This was the Catholic Church into which Thomas Merton was welcomed, and he quickly assumed the mantle of an avid true believer, criticizing other religious traditions, finding fault with his Episcopalian grandparents, and judging his younger brother's life. Prior to his becoming Catholic, Tom had suffered a long period of deep depression, guilt over his past life, and a sense of foreboding about the state of the world.[3] Following his baptism, he had replaced all his uncertainties and doubts with the clear knowledge that he was now part of the "one true church." In the current ecumenical atmosphere, it may be difficult to imagine the Catholic Church of the 1940s, and thus, the ambience of superiority that, to some degree, permeates Tom's account of John Paul's visit to Gethsemani. More importantly, it seems, we should pay attention to John Paul's background, so very different in formation from that of his brother, to learn, if we can, what kind of spiritual inspiration may have been at work in him.

Nascent Spirituality

Early Years

Throughout his life, John Paul carried within him a spirituality that, like a small but steady flame, shone in his actions: from his earliest years, he exuded a calming effect on others, and he had a determined sense of hope and a belief in the principle of fairness. As he matured, his spirituality became more expressive of his *law of love*, as Tom named it.

Even as an infant, John Paul exerted a positive effect on others. When put to bed in his upstairs room on Hillside Avenue, he would sing a melody that was heard by his parents and brother downstairs and caused them to

2. Shannon, "Note to the Reader," xxi.

3. Merton, T., *Seven Storey Mountain*, 214.

be still and to listen. His singing had a calming effect on his family, and this was to portend his lifestyle of caring for others.[4]

When John Paul was five years old, his brother and his friends threw rocks at him on multiple occasions to keep him away from their clubhouse. It was not fair that he was being excluded, but John Paul did not retaliate in kind, nor did he tattle or seek revenge. He displayed his disappointment in a way that Tom labeled a *law of love*, meaning, John Paul expected his brother to be concerned about him and to include him, because that was John Paul's own approach to Tom: he loved his older brother and sought to include him in his life.[5] When assaulted with a barrage of rocks thrown his way, John Paul simply stood his ground. His stance sent the message: *It doesn't matter what you do to me; I won't leave you.* No matter his brother's rejection, John Paul's love for Tom was steadfast.

In another incident from his childhood, John Paul courageously stared down and walked through a gang of approximately twenty-five older boys who were threatening his brother and his friends. The simple act of John Paul walking through the midst of that threatening gang to join his brother so defused the situation that the gang dissipated. Tom and his friends, the same kids who tried to drive John Paul away by throwing rocks at him, stood in awed silence. John Paul appeared in this moment to have no fear for his safety; instead, this five-year-old who had been rejected by his brother retained a calm confidence in his own safety, despite the threat that surrounded him. Without knowing his thoughts, an observer almost had to conclude that this youngster had an interior landscape very different from his brother, who was nearly 4 years older, and who, with his friends, fled the same threat in fear and holed up in a house, probably with a locked door.[6]

When Tom ignored John Paul during several summer vacations, John Paul made no response in kind; he continued to seek Tom's companionship. Likewise, when Owen Merton repeatedly left John Paul in the care of his grandparents, John Paul harbored no ill will toward his father; rather, he kept loving him. These two characteristics—forswearing revenge and maintaining connection to a person who has harmed you are the defining elements of the spirituality of forgiveness.

The psychological element of forgiveness involves the offended person dealing with his or her anger and resentment. The spiritual aspect involves

4. Merton, T., *Seven Storey Mountain*, 8.

5. Merton, T., *Seven Storey Mountain*, 23.

6. Merton, T., *Seven Storey Mountain*, 24.

avoiding an emotional separation from a harmful person and continually seeking their good. Both elements are clear in John Paul's character. Again and again throughout his formative years, John Paul reached out to connect with his brother. Again and again, he was rebuffed. As John Paul's visit to Gethsemani demonstrates, up until the last time he saw his brother Tom, he never stopped extending his hand in love.

Formal Religious Training

John Paul had been raised in the Episcopal faith, if only through church attendance on Easter and Christmas.[7] John Paul was known at Zion Episcopal Church in Douglaston: his maternal grandfather was a member of the vestry, a regular contributor, and a well-respected parishioner. The family respected all Protestant religions, and Mattie Jenkins would have spoken of her Quaker beliefs in the Jenkinses' home, as well.

According to the registry from the parish Book of Sacraments, John Paul had been baptized at Zion Episcopal Church when he was ten years old; as a student at The Choir School of St. John the Divine, John Paul was taught the meaning of the sacrament of Confirmation, which he received while a student, as well as basic beliefs of the Episcopal faith. He attended regular chapel services during his high school years at Gettysburg Academy, on the grounds of the Evangelical Lutheran Seminary of Pennsylvania. So, when John Paul told his brother at the outset of the Gethsemani visit that he did not know much about the church, he was referring to the Roman Catholic Church, for he had a long history of exposure to the Episcopal faith.

Maturing Spirituality

Of his college years, we know little of John Paul's spiritual growth; however, two events stand out as significant. The first is his interaction with a fraternity on campus to which he decided to pledge. Tom reports that John Paul was "pinned" by Sigma Alpha Epsilon, but that shortly afterward, he left the fraternity (Tom uses the phrase "ran away"), renting a house with

7. A factor that may have contributed to the Jenkins family sparse church attendance during John Paul's formative years was the destruction of the church by fire in 1924. For at least 2 years afterward, the Douglaston Episcopal community was without a church building. Another fire destroyed the choir room and sacristy in 1929. See Zion Episcopal Church History at https://zionepiscopal.org/about-us/history.

some other students.[8] Why did he leave the fraternity? Although Tom seemed to assume that the house John Paul rented in Ithaca was the scene of intense partying, no evidence is produced to that effect. Review of John Paul's transcript shows that his first year at Cornell, he took on the burden of six difficult courses, including two chemistry courses, mathematics, and French. There must have been something about fraternity life he did not like. Is it possible that, based on Tom's stories of his own fraternity at Columbia, John Paul questioned whether he could accomplish his academic goals under similar conditions? Hearing about fraternity life from Tom was one thing, but living it was something John Paul could not do. He decided to live by his own principles: he rejected the fraternity lifestyle.

The second event of interest occurred in June 1940, when Tom visited John Paul in Ithaca. It has been noted previously that Tom and John Paul, although brothers, spent their formative years in very different environments, often on completely different continents, influenced by people of fundamentally disparate ideas about the essential task of parenting. When reunited at the Jenkinses' family home in Douglaston after Tom was expelled from Clare College, these two young men were in many respects, strangers. It is, therefore, not surprising that in the few mentions of John Paul in his autobiography, *The Seven Storey Mountain*, Tom's portrayal of his interactions with his brother are devoid of the intimacy one would expect from brothers. Tom reports conversations with many other people during his time at Columbia and at St. Bonaventure, but only the interactions with John Paul are marked by a lack of dialogue. Nearly all of John Paul's responses in these scenes are reported as vague, nonspecific, and brief. The reader keeps waiting for the moment these two brothers open up to each other, for the intimate moment of mutual vulnerability. It never occurs, except perhaps in one flickering moment, when such intimacy appears as a potential, and is almost immediately snuffed out.

Tom's visit to Ithaca in June 1940 appears to have been an afterthought: he notes the "best thing" he can think of to do is to go to Olean where his friends are spending the summer, but that on his way there, he will visit his brother in Ithaca.[9] In fact, Ithaca lies between New York City and Olean. Today, with all the improvements in the highway system since 1940, it is still four to five hours from New York to Ithaca by car, and Olean is another two hours beyond Ithaca. By Tom's own telling, he himself never takes a

8. Merton, T., *Seven Storey Mountain*, 151.

9. Merton, T., *Seven Storey Mountain*, 287.

trip solely to spend time with John Paul, whereas John Paul makes trips to see Tom after visiting Mexico and during his leave from the RCAF (prior to embarking to England), that had only one purpose in mind: to spend a dedicated period of time with his brother.

During the June 1940 visit, Tom notes he spent only a couple of days in Ithaca. Tom reports his observation that John Paul's life is made up of "reckless peregrinations" between the university and the town, and he relates that on his last morning there, John Paul accompanied him to attend Mass.[10] We never learn from Tom of anything that is meaningful to John Paul, no mention of John Paul's integration into the Miscall family, his exploration of photography, concerns about the war, or his thoughts about how he might volunteer for the military. As Tom's comments about his brother are consistently critical in a negative sense, we may assume that his verbal interactions with John Paul were similar. If John Paul *had been* exploring a spiritual landscape and had questions about Catholicism that Tom might have been able to answer, would he have risked a conversation that may have led to criticism of this most intimate longing? Would he confess his deep desire for God to Tom, who repeatedly judged his brother as falling short of standards Tom held dear?

When the two brothers attend Mass on that morning in June 1940, Tom reports that John Paul knelt during the Mass alongside Tom and watched as Tom received the Eucharist. After the Mass, a moment occurs unique in *The Seven Storey Mountain*: Tom reports that John Paul "told me he had been talking to the chaplain of the Catholic students."[11] Here is the moment of vulnerability, in which John Paul is reported—for the first and only time in this book—to have told his brother something that comes from deep within, something secret, hidden: in the context of the shared liturgical experience, he offers that he has been talking to a priest.

There is no further report of continued dialogue. Instead, Tom remarks that he cannot tell if John Paul is truly attracted to "the faith, or the fact that the chaplain was interested in flying."[12] He ends the report of his visit to his brother by stating that he has learned John Paul has been taking regular flying lessons in Ithaca.

For those of us who have at one time longed for a meaningful exchange with a certain person, but who have experienced repeated rebuffs

10. Merton, T., *Seven Storey Mountain*, 287.

11. Merton, T., *Seven Storey Mountain*, 287.

12. Merton, T., *Seven Storey Mountain*, 287.

in some regard, it requires little effort to imagine that John Paul, proffering one piece of information about his spiritual life, hoped his brother Tom would open the door a bit wider with some gentle encouragement for him to reveal more. Based on Tom's statement that he cannot discern John Paul's true interest—faith or flying—it sounds like Tom's insensitivity to the import of the moment resulted in shutting the door instead.

In the autumn of 1940, John Paul traveled to Mexico after he was expelled from Cornell. On his return to New York in May 1941, he visited his brother in Olean, New York. During this visit, Tom again asked John Paul what he thought about becoming a Catholic. John Paul said he had thought a little about it.[13] In this exchange, we see that John Paul has resorted to the same brief and vague response that we hear throughout the book. For example, in summer 1940, Tom is surprised to run into his brother on Church Street in Manhattan at a time when John Paul was supposed to be at school in Ithaca.[14] When he asks John Paul what he's doing in New York City, John Paul asks a question in turn: has Tom heard of the new "scheme" the U.S. Navy uses to attract recruits? Throughout the entire exchange, by Tom's reporting, John Paul does not actually tell Tom his purpose for being in New York. Tom surmises John Paul is there enlisting in the Navy, but John Paul is not reported as actually telling Tom so. Throughout *The Seven Storey Mountain*, John Paul's responses to Tom are reported as short and nonspecific, and for the most part, except in that one time, after the two brothers had attended Mass, John Paul never reveals anything of true importance in his life. After John Paul returned from Mexico, Tom concluded John Paul was not interested in Catholicism. Tom assumed John Paul was aimless and unhappy because he did not have the grace of the sacraments in the Catholic Church.[15]

Tom assumed John Paul's life was similar to his own before the change of heart that sparked Tom's interest in Catholicism. Tom had been depressed, felt guilty about his licentious behavior, and had a sense of foreboding about the state of the world. However, John Paul was not deeply depressed, feeling remorse for his past life, nor was he dejected by the state of the world. If he appeared aimless or dejected it was because of the situational factors of his life: no college degree and no clear work path.

13. Merton, T., *Seven Storey Mountain*, 335.
14. Merton, T., *Seven Storey Mountain*, 299.
15. Merton, T., *Seven Storey Mountain*, 397.

Baptism at Gethsemani

Photo by the author of monastery enclosure at the Abbey of Gethsemani.

When John Paul had finished his RCAF training, he took a leave to visit family. John Paul's first stop was to see his Uncle Harold, who had married Elsie Hauck Holahan, who had been caretaker and companion for Mattie Jenkins. In 1941, Harold took a job with the engineering firm of John W. Harris Associates at Sixteenth Street NW in Washington, D.C. Harold and Elsie lived at 4525 North Chelsea Lane in the affluent Washington D.C. suburb of Bethesda.[16] Part of John Paul's reason for visiting his uncle was to inform Harold that in his will, John Paul had left Harold his share of the joint properties he and Harold owned at Stone Island, Maine, Douglas Manor, Long Island, New York, and at Coral Gables, Florida.[17]

Following his visit to Harold and Elsie, John Paul boarded the Chesapeake and Ohio flagship passenger train, the *George Washington*, at Union Station in Washington D.C. for the trip to Louisville, Kentucky. From there, an hour bus ride took him to Bardstown, Kentucky, and a twenty-minute cab ride to the Abbey of Gethsemani.

The abbey is part of the Order of Cistercians of the Strict Observance (OCSO) known as Trappists. Trappist monks live a silent life of prayer and work. Monks take vows of *obedience* to an abbot, *stability* (the promise

16. U.S. World War II Draft Registration Cards (1942).

17. Stanley, "Pigeon, Caged, Drowns," 33.

to live out their lives in one community), and *conversion of manners* (the promise to live a monastic life of poverty, celibacy, silence, manual labor, and separation from the world of the dominant culture). Tom arrived at Gethsemani and entered the community on December 13, 1941, as a postulant; he became a novice on February 21, 1942.[18]

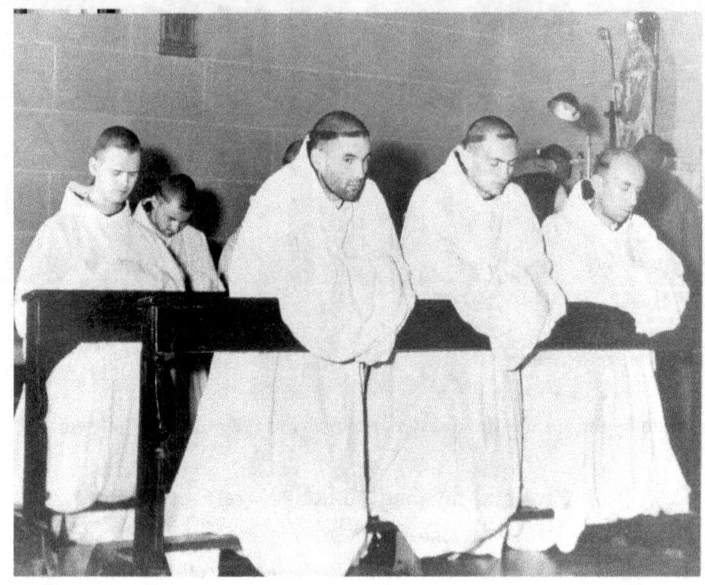

Thomas Merton as novice, in prayer (far right), circa 1942. Used with permission of the Merton Legacy Trust and the Thomas Merton Center at Bellarmine University.

As the cab from the bus station turned left from Monk's Road onto the grounds of the monastery, the first thing John Paul saw was the monastic enclosure: a ten-foot stone wall encompassing the property and preventing access by anyone other than the monks. As the cab drove slowly down the tree-lined road, the gatehouse entrance for visitors came into view. Above the entrance door is a lintel stone with the engraving *Pax Intrantibus:* Peace to All Who Enter Here.

18. Mott, *Seven Mountains of Thomas Merton*, 211.

The inscription in Latin over the gatehouse entrance to the Abbey of Gethsemani reads, "Peace to All Who Enter Here." Used with permission of the Abbey of Gethsemani, Trappist, Kentucky.

Tom met John Paul in the gatehouse. Tom stood five feet, eight inches tall and wore a white robe, white scapular, and white band tied around his waist. John Paul was almost six feet tall and wore his blue RCAF uniform with its Air Observer Brevet over the left breast pocket, RCAF cap worn slightly to the right side, and sergeant stripes on his sleeves. The brothers were each in garb that exemplified their unique differences: Tom, contemplative; John Paul, a man of action.

When Tom met John Paul at the guesthouse, Tom wondered if John Paul had decided whether to enter the Catholic Church. As Tom reports, he began to ask if John Paul did not want to be baptized into the Catholic Church. The way Tom reports this conversation raises questions. It appears that John Paul acquiesced to Tom's zealous desire to see him baptized merely to please his brother; however, a closer examination of the text suggests John Paul may have been traveling his own road to this decision, and that his visit to Gethsemani merely provided the opportunity for something he'd been wanting for some time.

The text of Tom's autobiography provides ample examples of John Paul dodging Tom's queries, demonstrating he did not reveal his interior life to Tom. It seems unlikely that John Paul would have agreed to the baptism into Catholicism during his visit to Gethsemani only because Tom wanted or pressured him into it. John Paul's exploration of several ways to enter the military and eventual enlistment in Canadian armed forces, against his brother's wishes, is evidence that he made his own decisions. However, he must have explored Catholicism with someone. Two likely influences included people he knew in Ithaca: Father Cleary, the Catholic chaplain at the university, and the Miscall family.

There exists no record that indicates John Paul and Fr. Cleary discussed the potential of John Paul becoming a catechumen. The only clue we have is his statement in June 1940 to Tom that he had been talking to the priest. Several sources were explored to learn if the Miscall family were Catholics. John Paul so valued his adopted family that of the three visits he made on his leave before shipping out to England (to Harold Jenkins, to Tom at Gethsemani, and to the Miscall family), a visit to their home was the last, during which he made out his will and assigned his treasured possessions to members of the Miscall family. It seems possible that matters of faith and morality could have been discussed in the manner that John Paul so appreciated at the Miscall household, and that these discussions could have influenced his own spiritual journey. Leonard Miscall's father was a baptized Catholic, as well as his brother Darwin. Baptism for Len could not be confirmed. However, there is evidence that the Miscall's son Jack, who was in grade school when John Paul was introduced into the family, was also a baptized Catholic. After extensive research, no evidence has been found that Leonard or his wife Rovene were practicing Catholics, but clearly there was a Christian, if not Catholic, ethos expressed as a warmth and inclusiveness that attracted John Paul such that he allowed himself to be unofficially adopted as a member of their family. John Stanley, who interviewed the Miscalls, emphasized that John Paul valued the open, honest discussion of ideas at their dinner table.[19] It's easy to imagine that with the war building in Europe and United States involvement pending, this would have generated in John Paul a conflict between his desire to serve and his awareness of his family's consistent opposition to participating in war and the killing of others. Honest discussion of the morality of war necessarily generates some soul searching; we can assume that dialogue with Len and

19. Stanley, "Pigeon, Caged, Drowns," 39.

Rovene (Len Miscall ultimately served in the U.S. Navy as a Captain in the Corps of Engineers) and witnessing their loving concern for those around them, including John Paul himself, served as a powerful influence for good in John Paul. While it seems highly unlikely that John Paul would agree to baptism in the Catholic Church merely because Tom proposed it, it seems very probable that by the time he reached the door to the abbey at Gethsemani there had been stirrings in his soul for some time. It seems more likely that his visit to Gethsemani was the culmination of many events and interventions, and that at that very moment, he was so poised to accept God's grace that Tom's question about baptism was all it required to allow that grace to work in him. The very fact that of all the books Tom brought him, it was *The Story of a Soul* to which he was attracted is an indication of both his interior state and God's Providence, for who better to describe to him the experience of God's sustaining love than St. Thérèse? That he read it, as Tom puts it, "all in one gulp," indicates something of how hungry he was for the message she conveyed. In describing her "little way," Thérèse told that every evening at dinner, she lovingly escorted a particularly vexatious elderly nun from chapel to the dinner table; surely John Paul recognized his own actions mirroring hers as he doggedly reached in love toward his brother, only to be rebuffed year after year.

One thing is certain: John Paul willingly participated in the process of becoming a Roman Catholic. He knew little of the faith and he needed instruction in Catholicism's basic beliefs before baptism. Tom spoke with his novice master, Father Robert McGann, who suggested Tom instruct John Paul as much as possible and give him books about Catholicism to read. John Paul was also able to attend a weekend retreat being given by Father James Fox, the retreat master for the monastery guests.[20] Several of the priests recommended books for him to read, and the retreat master held private conferences with him. Father Fox and Father Francis (guest master and librarian) provided books on spirituality: *The Story of a Soul* by St. Thérèse of Lisieux, and *Imitation of Christ* by Thomas à Kempis. Tom added the *Catechism of the Council of Trent* (a sixteenth century response to Protestantism). The concepts of faith and grace filled much of the content about which Tom spoke. All of this was done with the approval of the abbot, Dom Frederic Dunne; although, he said it was not possible to baptize John Paul at the monastery (the monastery does not initiate catechumens).

20. Fox, "Spiritual Son," 143.

During the visit, Tom vividly remembered his past relationship with John Paul and all the many harmful things he had done that he now regretted. His recollection of their twenty-year history flooded his consciousness with the realization of how separated he had been from John Paul. In Tom's mind, their relationship was compared to a car accident in which the victims needed to be revived.[21] That metaphor implies the relationship between the brothers is dead. Tom was so sure of this fact that he wrote with certitude that John Paul could not have come to Gethsemani "merely" to see him. Given the past, Tom felt it would be natural that John Paul would not want to visit his brother, which may have been an accurate assumption for some people; however, his assumption did not fit the way John Paul felt, which was clearly demonstrated by John Paul's desire to make the trek to Kentucky to visit Tom. In 1943, there was no interstate system or widespread commercial air service; thus, getting to Bardstown, Kentucky was a long train ride with many stops at small towns along the way. It was not convenient to Washington, D. C, where John Paul had first stopped to visit Harold. Further, it was yet another agonizingly long train ride from Louisville, Kentucky, to Ithaca, New York, to the Miscalls, his last stop on this leave. In the metaphor of the auto accident victims, healing required medical treatment. For Tom himself, healing his relationship with John Paul required reconciliation. It is likely, however, that if asked, John Paul would have denied the need for apologies from Tom, since, based on his obvious desire to see his older brother, his love for Tom had never wavered.

The act of reconciliation requires four actions on the part of the person who has harmed another: 1) apologize (a sincere, not a pro forma, apology), 2) accept total responsibility for the acts committed, 3) pledge no further similar acts will occur, and 4) make amends in some way to the person harmed.[22]

For Tom, steeped in the teachings and rubrics of the Roman Catholic Church, this would bring to his mind the sacrament of Penance (now named Sacrament of Reconciliation). In this sacrament, a person (the penitent) speaks privately to a priest (the priest is the sign and instrument of God's merciful love for the sinner), recounts his/her offenses (sins), acknowledges he or she was wrong, declares sorrow for his/her actions (by reciting the Act of Contrition), promises life changes that include committing this act (sin) no more, and agrees to do penance.

21. Merton, T., *Seven Storey Mountain*, 396.
22. Worthington, *Forgiveness and Reconciliation*, 194–220.

In the secular world, following injury, these are the same elements for the process of reconciliation: a person sincerely apologizes to the person he or she has harmed, names the things for which he or she accepts full responsibility, pledges not to repeat these acts, and makes some effort to atone for the injury inflicted.

Tom comments that he has "atoned" for all the harm he has done to his brother, the evil he committed, and that he was absolved from his wrongdoing by instructing John Paul for baptism.[23] Tom must have felt he had done his penance through the exhaustion of four days of instruction to his brother. In his mind he was now healed, absolved, and reconciled to his brother without having expressed an apology, naming the things he did to hurt his brother, or promising not to repeat the acts. He demonstrates his own very limited understanding of himself and of the Gospel message to "bring one's offering to the altar" only after reconciling with those one has injured. Thomas Merton, although he later became the mystic we know and think of today, started his spiritual journey like the rest of us, trying to find his authentic self, and at the time of writing *The Seven Storey Mountain*, he was still searching.

And yet, characteristic of John Paul, he had long ago forgiven Tom his mean, neglectful behavior. John Paul never harbored any ill will toward Tom. John Paul had never ceased to seek a relationship with Tom. He came to Gethsemani to visit his brother whom he loved, knowing he was going to war and probably his death, to say goodbye, to reminisce and remember family stories, and simply be present to Tom. John Paul was not inclined to be fault-finding. His widow, Margaret Evans Merton Kirkman (she remarried in 1946) later described him in a letter of August 15, 1975 to John Stanley as a serene man who never criticized or judged his family. John Paul's agenda was solely fraternal; Tom's agenda was his brother's baptism. For John Paul, there was no sense of urgency to be baptized; John Paul was not in the same place as Tom had been before his baptism: seriously depressed and filled with remorse. At the time he visited Tom at Gethsemani, John Paul was an accomplished airman, with a sense of purpose and direction in his life. He saw where he could do some good, and he had prepared himself for the task.

On July 26, 1943, John Paul was baptized at St. Catherine's Catholic church in New Haven, Kentucky.[24] A parishioner stood in as a sponsor. A

---

23. Merton, T., *Seven Storey Mountain*, 398.

24. John Paul's Certificate of Baptism from St. Catherine Church is housed in the

curious fact about the baptism is that records of the Cathedral of St. John the Divine in New York City show John Paul Merton was confirmed there in 1931. In the Episcopal faith, baptism would have had to precede the sacrament of Confirmation. Canon Law of the Roman Catholic Church states that a previous Christian Baptism would have been acknowledged as valid. Both John Paul and Tom may not have recalled the prior baptism or may not have had a sufficient understanding of it. Or more likely, the clergy were playing it safe, and the baptism at St. Catherine would have been a conditional baptism, done in the instance where there is uncertainty regarding the validity of the non-Catholic baptism.

The next day, in Our Lady of Victories Chapel at the monastery, John Paul received the Eucharist at the Mass celebrated by Abbot Frederick Dunne, with his brother Tom as altar server. Tom reported that he was worried John Paul would not be able to find his way from the retreat house to the chapel, and so he rushed to the chapel ahead of Reverend Father to see if John Paul had made the journey there. When he entered the church, he saw his brother at the end of the nave, in the empty tribune, or balcony (the only part of the church where visitors were permitted to attend Mass; in the current church, visitors are permitted into the nave of the church).[25]

Thomas Merton Center, Bellarmine University, Louisville, Kentucky.

25. Merton, T., *Seven Storey Mountain*, 394–99.

Photo of the church nave taken from the tribune or balcony circa 1942. The church has been renovated to a simpler style. Used with permission of the Abbey of Gethsemani, Trappist, Kentucky.

John Paul was kneeling in the tribune when Tom saw him.

In the Episcopal Church, kneeling is "a traditional posture of prayer" that expresses "supplication, and humility."[26] In the modern Episcopal Church, kneeling is practiced during Lent and on Easter, but in John Paul's day, it would have been part of every liturgy.

That Tom finds John Paul kneeling is significant, for John Paul entered the balcony alone, and in that solitude, he knelt. No liturgy was ongoing, for which he may have been directed to kneel. Instead, he adopted the posture voluntarily. Kneeling in solitude usually comes from an inner desire to connect with God, and an awareness of the nature of our human condition in the presence of the divine. It is an almost automatic act, given that awareness. It is an outward sign of an interior process at work, and in this case, suggests it may not have been the first time John Paul knelt in communion with God.

26. "Kneel."

Conclusion

John Paul needed no baptism into the Christian faith for he had already been baptized in the Episcopal faith and had lived a life infused by the grace of that sacrament. Outside the monastery walls, John Paul and Tom had spent only a few years together and shared hardly any interests in common. Now, their shared faith was a platform from which the brothers might develop a closeness at least in the realm of their spiritual journeys. It was not to occur. As John Paul waved to Tom from the cab taking him to the bus station, both brothers knew this might be the last time they would see each other. And so it was.

9

Wartime in England

After leaving his brother at Gethsemani, John Paul's next stop was a farewell visit to the Miscalls in Ithaca, New York. On August 4, 1942, John Paul made out his last will and testament.[1] The will was witnessed by Elizabeth R. Brown, Audrey Lunn, and Abraham W. Feinberg (friend and attorney). To Len Miscall, now a Lieutenant Commander in the U.S. Navy, and his wife, Rovene, John Paul left his books, records, Russian wolfhound, and car. He named Abraham Feinberg, his friend and attorney, and Rovene Miscall as executors of the will. John Paul left for England with a trail of wishes that had not been fulfilled: to enter the childhood clubhouse of his brother, to earn a college degree, to be a pilot, and finally, to join his own country's armed forces. He did not brood over these unfulfilled dreams. He was not one to ruminate over disappointments. He was an optimist and paid attention to the present moment, to what was going right in his life.

He was off to war!

John Paul, not yet twenty-four years old, left Halifax, Nova Scotia, on August 7, 1942 for a transatlantic voyage, the same journey he had taken four times in his childhood.[2] Instead of the White Star ocean liner, he had passage on a troop ship, and instead of fellow passengers who were tourists, there were hundreds of other servicemen going off to war. This trip took

1. The Last Will and Testament of John Paul Merton is housed in The Thomas Merton Center, Bellarmine University, Louisville, Kentucky.

2. Unless otherwise noted, all information in this chapter is from John Paul Merton's unpaginated RCAF record: Ottawa, Canada, Library and Archives, "WWII Service Files of War Dead (1939–1947)."

him through the waters familiar in his youth, now infested with German U-boats. He was exactly where he wanted to be: on his way with thousands of others to fight the war in Europe.

As the war progressed, the German Navy increased production of submarines, and German U-boat patrols of the North Atlantic intensified, searching for, and sinking, as many vessels as possible. One convoy from Halifax in the patrolled zone lost nine ships to German submarines. In 1942, the losses of Allied convoys increased significantly so that the Allies adjusted their patrols and protection of North Atlantic convoys.

The dangers of war were real. John Paul knew the dangers but confronting them would have filled him with both fear and exhilaration. He was going to do something to help: his life finally had meaning. He went into the future with faith and a longstanding attachment to family. He was living out the law of love in this new way.

Following the perilous trip across the Atlantic, on August 18, 1942, the troop ship navigated through the Liverpool Bay, into the Mersey River, and finally docked at Liverpool. From there, John Paul was transported to the Royal Air Force unit at Hurn in Bournemouth, Dorset, for processing. He was headed for his next training assignment at Operational Training Unit Number 16, in Upper-Heyford, Oxfordshire. First, though, he had a disembarkation leave, so he decided to spend time in London.

Training in England

The London of 1942 was not the place he had seen as a child. Then he was with his grandparents with whom he could share his thoughts and questions. Now it was a bombed-out city, devastated by the blitzkrieg. Buildings were sandbagged, the stone and bricks of bombed and ruined buildings blocked the streets, and electricity was limited. Unlike when he was a seven-year-old child, he now had an acute sense of loneliness: he had no one close with whom he could share this experience. A chance meeting[3] with a young lady wearing the uniform of the Auxiliary Territorial Service,[4] the women's branch of the British Army, was to change that.

Beginning in September 1940, the Luftwaffe had bombed London and other British cities, culminating in the blitz of the first eight days of May 1941, when the cities of Birkenhead and Liverpool (in the county of Mersey

3. Stanley, "Pigeon, Caged, Drowns," 12.
4. Research Information of the ATS, "Auxiliary Territorial Service."

on the west coast of England) were targeted.[5] The woman wearing the ATS uniform whom he would later marry was from Birkenhead and had lived through the blitz. Birkenhead is a seaport town on the Wirral peninsula across the Mersey River from Liverpool. The docks of Birkenhead are part of the port of Liverpool, the largest port on the west coast of England, and were an important target for the Luftwaffe due to the vital imports of food and supplies received from the United States and Canada. During the blitz in May 1941, 681 German bombers dropped 350 tons of high explosives on Birkenhead and Liverpool. In Merseyside, 1,900 people were killed, 1,450 seriously wounded, and 70,000 made homeless.[6]

From the middle of September until December 1942, John Paul was stationed at Operational Training Unit Number 16, where bomber crews were trained to perform nighttime bombing runs. Gunnery and navigation training were key elements in the plan to focus on nighttime bombing sorties on the European continent from the English coast. The Vickers Wellington aircraft used by the RAF for bombing had a newly designed, geodesic, aluminum alloy frame covered with doped and varnished linen that made the plane lightweight, sturdy, and durable.[7]

While at the Operational Training Unit, John Paul visited Oxford and enjoyed seeing the city, the bookstores, and the various colleges. He wrote to his brother to tell him about the city of Oxford, and Tom had no trouble interpreting the words that had been blocked out by the military censors.[8] It is possible he visited Merton College at Oxford University and may have mistakenly associated its name with his own surname.

In the autumn of 1942, John Paul visited his father's sister, Aunt Gwynedd, most likely, taking the train from Waterloo Station to Horsley Station.[9] No doubt he would have preferred to drive (he had bought a road map of England's countryside). Gwynedd lived with her husband, Erwin Trier, in Fairlawn, West Horsley, Surrey. The Triers had two sons, Richard and Frank, both of whom served with British forces; Richard was eventually taken prisoner of war in Italy.[10]

---

5. "Blitz"; "Liverpool Blitz."

6. "Blitz."

7. Wallis, "Geodetics."

8. Merton, T., *Seven Storey Mountain*, 399.

9. Stanley, "Pigeon, Caged, Drowns," 49.

10. U.K. Allied Prisoners of War (1939–1945).

During John Paul's free time, he wrote letters to the younger Walter Hauck (the brother of Elsie Hauck Jenkins) of whom he was fond.[11] John Paul wrote several letters to his brother Tom (in November 1942 he told Tom of his wedding plans). When he did not have a pass for the weekend, he read novels, including *Night Train to Berlin,* as well as Spanish novels with the help of a translation dictionary. After his death, his effects were found to contain a copy of the Gospel of St. Luke.[12]

During training, John Paul met Bob Hart, a fellow Air Observer in his squadron, at Operational Training Unit Number 16, according to Mark Charnley, who was a friend of Hart (email of July 4, 2018 to the author). Later, they were roommates in the squadron barracks at RAF Kirmington. Each was dating a woman in the Auxiliary Territorial Service: Hart dated Beryl Jones and John Paul dated Margaret May Evans. Hart planned to wait until after the war to marry. John Paul, or "Mert" as he was known by his squadron mates, was already planning to marry Margaret May. Together, Hart and John Paul spent time in the pub known as *Marrowbone and Cleaver,* the village pub nicknamed by the airmen as *The Chopper,* where John Paul would have been teased for being a "Yank"[13] or insulted because Americans failed to get into the war sooner. By now the "wildman of Gettysburg Academy" was tamed; his response would have been a humorous reply. The sobering effects of both military training and war, and the change of spirit resulting from his recent baptism in the Catholic Church had mellowed him.

Finally, as December 1942 came to an end, training for John Paul was complete. Instructors thought he showed weapon firing results better than average; he was judged to be consistent, reliable, and careful about weapons maintenance. The navigation training results were initially disappointing, but he improved with practice; overall, his instructors judged that he had average ability because he worked hard. He was noted to have a good working relationship with the navigator. John Paul was assigned to RAF Kirmington, Lincolnshire.

11. Copies of letters written by John Paul Merton to the younger Walter Hauck, his brother Thomas, and others are housed at the Thomas Merton Center, Bellarmine University, Louisville, Kentucky.

12. John Paul's personal effects from his locker are detailed in his service file.

13. "Yank" is slang for "Yankee," originally a term used to describe only a native or inhabitant of New England (circa mid-1700s), but later for a native or inhabitant of the United States.

The operational tour of any airman at that time required thirty flight missions or sorties, which took about three to four months. Having finalized an operational tour, an airman could be assigned to a training unit to train new aircrew. Most airmen never lived to train new recruits. In March 1943, the life expectancy of Royal Air Force bomber crews was two weeks. By the war's end, Bomber Command recorded 57,205 men killed or missing in action, 8,403 wounded, and 9,838 taken as prisoners of war. This represented 60 percent of the operational crews that flew during the war.[14]

John Paul had completed more than a year of training. He was now a skilled and well-trained airman. Training had instilled confidence and a sense of duty and mission, and he looked forward to getting into the battle. He also looked forward to marrying the woman he had been courting throughout the months since he met her in London on his arrival in England.

Courtship and Marriage

In 1939, England was struggling with a loss of its workforce and limited food supplies due to the war. Farms were at risk for lying fallow as the farm workers were in uniform. In June 1939, the British government renewed the Women's Land Army, which had been halted after WWI. Women from all over the country worked the farms while the farmers (men) enrolled in the armed forces. The Women's Land Army was a voluntary unit until passage in December 1941 of the National Service Act, requiring unmarried women to serve in an auxiliary service. By 1943, most English women were involved in some sort of active service in the war effort.[15]

Margaret, a city person, would not have wanted to work on a farm; she wanted to contribute to the war effort in a more direct manner, and this is the reason she volunteered for the Auxiliary Territorial Service. John Paul was on leave in London in September 1942,[16] at the same time that Margaret was in London taking tests for a special branch of wireless work. She eventually qualified for a highly specialized intelligence assignment at Kedleston Hall, North Lincolnshire.[17] The work of the unit was to intercept and analyze enemy radio transmissions. Any encrypted messages were

14. "WW2: Could You Be Part."
15. "Women in Uniform."
16. Stanley, "Pigeon, Caged, Drowns," 12.
17. Stanley, "Pigeon, Caged, Drowns," 12.

forwarded to Bletchley Park, the top-secret facility for code breaking for further analysis (where Alan Turing cracked the German U-boat Enigma cipher).[18] Once selected for the assignment, she underwent training in Wiltshire before reporting to Kedleston Hall, Derbyshire. Kedleston Hall was a large mansion that was part of the Courzon family ancestral country estate; the Courzons had provided the estate to the Royal Air Force for the duration of the war.[19]

Both John Paul and Margaret were bound by the Official Secrets Acts: Margaret was not permitted to speak of her intelligence work, and he could not speak of his bombing missions, but this did not prevent their growing intimacy. In the following autumn months, when John Paul got weekend passes, he traveled from Upper-Heyford to Wiltshire, where Margaret was in training, a distance of about ninety miles. In September 1942, they celebrated her twenty-first birthday. By October, they had fallen in love. In November, they celebrated his twenty-fourth birthday. In whatever way they thought of celebrating Christmas, when they spoke of the war they probably wished, as most of the English did, "the war will be over by Christmas."

Fortunately, the specifics of the first meeting between John Paul and Margaret are not lost to history. In a letter to John Stanley[20] dated May 14, 1975, Margaret wrote of John Paul and their relationship:

> He was six feet tall, possibly a little more and was so fair his hair was almost white and he had blue eyes. He was a most gentle man, with a wonderful smile and an air of complete serenity. He appreciated beautiful things and as his Father had found expression in painting, I think John had his in photography.
>
> We had only one evening of each other's company. He told me he was an American in the RCAF and we chatted very generally about books, music, hobbies, etc. and he asked if I would correspond with him. This we did and I gathered he was a keen photographer and one who was interested in people and places. Whilst I was training in Wiltshire he came there for a couple of days in October. We had a day in Bath and he took numerous photographs and was interested in its history. He told me his parents

---

18. See the Bletchley Park Museum website at https://bletchleypark.org.uk/.

19. "Kedleston Hall."

20. John Stanley had been a monk in the Abbey of Gethsemani with Thomas Merton. Stanley later left the monastery. He wrote an unpublished biography of John Paul Merton entitled "The Pigeon, Caged, Drowns," for which he corresponded with Margaret May Merton Kirkman.

were dead and he was brought up by his maternal grandparents. His father, he said, had been a painter and he had a brother.

We fell in love and it was only when John spoke of marriage I learned he was a Roman Catholic and he told me of his conversion and of Tom being a Trappist monk. John was so happy in his new faith but it posed a problem for marriage, as I was Church of England. I told him I would not change my faith in order to marry him but was willing to see the parish priest to ask if a dispensation could be arranged. The priest asked many questions on my religious views, my knowledge of the Bible and told me my responsibilities should a dispensation be granted. He complimented me on my principles and then shocked me by asking if I was sure John was a bachelor!! This same wonderful man married us on 23rd Feb 1943.

In Margaret, John Paul finally had someone who was as anxious to be with him as he was to be with her, an attachment for which he had yearned his entire life. There would be no more acute loneliness. John Paul and Margaret had spoken of marriage in the autumn. Their plan to live in the United States after the war was the easy part to imagine. They planned to live in Ithaca, and, in all probability, John Paul planned to work as a photographer, the occupation he had listed on his RCAF enlistment papers. At that time, Margaret's skills in intelligence gathering would have made her a candidate for employment in research or many other jobs that could utilize her intelligence training.

Margaret belonged to the Church of England but agreed to marriage in the Catholic Church. If they were to be married in the Catholic Church a dispensation was necessary so that John Paul could marry a non-Catholic. Margaret agreed to speak to the Catholic priest in Birkenhead, Father William Cannon Griffin, who met with her and explored her commitment to her faith. Father Griffin was impressed with her depth of faith, agreed to marry them, and advised Margaret of what would be expected of her in an interdenominational marriage. As a non-Catholic, at that time, she was required to promise to raise any children from the marriage as Catholic. In addition, she was told that the marriage ceremony had to be conducted in the rectory or a place within the church other than within the sanctuary of the church (Canon 1124 of the current code requires only the Catholic partner to promise to raise the children as Catholic)[21].

21. "Do Catholic Parents Have to Raise Their Children as Catholic?"

John Paul spoke with Father George Brewster, the priest from the Catholic parish of The Immaculate Conception at Bicester, assigned to service for the Royal Air Force in Kirmington, and he agreed to submit the application for a dispensation to marry a non-Catholic. Archbishop Leighton Williams granted the dispensation. John Paul requested and was granted a five-day leave.

Margaret and John Paul were married on Tuesday, February 23, 1943, in St. Laurence Roman Catholic Church in Birkenhead, Cheshire, by Father Griffin.[22]

Margaret's father, John Albert Kay Evans, walked her down the aisle to where John Paul stood, as a sign that she was beginning a new life with her husband and leaving her life in her nuclear family (Margaret's mother had died when Margaret was six years old). The witnesses to the ceremony were recorded as William Owen and Ruth Evans. To Margaret's surprise, the marriage was inside the church sanctuary, not in the rectory, as Father Griffin had warned it would be, but without organ music. Perhaps if the ceremony had too closely resembled a Catholic celebration of the sacrament of marriage, it would have drawn attention to the fact that Father Griffin had bent the rules.

22. England and Wales, Civil Registration Marriage Index (1916–2005).

John Paul Merton and Margaret May Evans on the steps of St. Laurence Church, Birkenhead, England, February 23, 1943, the day they were married. Used with permission of the Merton Legacy Trust and the Thomas Merton Center at Bellarmine University.

It is not known if there was a reception following the ceremony; it would have been a challenge due to the rationing of food, which began in January 1940. Among other things, the British were limited to four ounces of ham and bacon, two ounces of butter, three pints of milk, and one egg per week, hardly enough to make a cake. By May 1942, restaurants and hotels were restricted in their meal service to only one course of meat, poultry, or fish, and cost could be no more than five shillings.[23]

23. Barrow, "Food Rationing."

Immediately following the ceremony, they left for a honeymoon in Grasmere, a village in the Lake District. In her May 14, 1975 letter to John Stanley, Margaret wrote of their marriage and honeymoon:

> I had asked if we might have the services of an organist and learned after, he (Rev Griffin) had told a white lie in saying the organ was out of order. He also married us in the body of the church which was not usual in a mixed marriage.
>
> Our honeymoon was spent in Grasmere, the home of Wordsworth. Although it was February, it was the mildest winter in years. We walked for miles taking photographs, visiting beauty spots and making plans with youthful confidence of home in America when the war was over. I was never to see him again.

John Paul had considerable assets, and he was not frugal when it came to money. Probably at Margaret's instigation, she and John Paul set up a joint bank account at the Chase National Bank, where they planned to save their money for a life in America after the war.

John Paul had arrived at RAF Kirmington, Lincolnshire, in early January 1943 to join the 155 Squadron, which disbanded two weeks after he joined. While with the 155 Squadron, he flew seven missions: night raids and operations to lay mines in the sea. He was then assigned to the 166 Squadron, whose mission was to lay mines in enemy waters and to do night bombing over enemy territory. He was assigned to the crew of Flying Officer Jacques Lupton (pilot) as the Air Observer or Bomb Aimer. John Paul flew six sorties with Lupton and the 166 Squadron before a fateful mission to Mannheim, Germany.

During this period, two incidents appear in his service record that would be more readily understood if more detail had been provided. On February 16, 1943, he was reprimanded for disclosing information contrary to regulations. Did he mistakenly tell Margaret about the timing of a mission as it related to their wedding plans? We cannot know. The second reprimand occurred one month later when, on March 9, 1943, he failed to report for night flying. Did he get delayed after a trip to see his new wife? Again, there are no details to clarify this incident.

During the war, the 166 Squadron lost fifty-one Wellington bombers flying from Kirmington.[24] Bombers flying from this base were part of the Ruhr Valley campaign of the British Command, beginning March 1943 with the raid on Essen. They joined RAF squadron 617 which flew from

24. "Kirmington Airfield History."

Scrampton in the audacious bombing raid known as the Dambusters Raid on May 16–17, 1943.[25] Striking the industrial heartland of Hitler's army was of paramount importance: the purpose was to deprive the German army of necessary oil, chemical works, communication facilities, and fuel supplies. Initially, sorties occurred in daytime, but the RAF lacked sufficient air defense for the squadrons. The bombers only had forward and tail turret guns, leaving the plane vulnerable to attack on all sides of its fuselage. In addition, bombing raids at night were the only means the British had at this time since they had no allies on the ground in Europe. By late 1941, the British had given up target bombing and began a policy of area, or carpet, bombing.

The 166 Squadron went out on a mission on April 14, 1943, and among the twelve planes in the squadron were those of Sergeant Bob Hart and Sergeant John Paul Merton. Hart's plane went down with no indication of survivors. John Paul's plane dropped its payload and returned to the airbase. Once the circumstances of the loss of Hart's plane were clear to John Paul, he immediately wrote to Beryl, Hart's fiancée, to tell her that Hart would return. Mark Charnley, Hart's friend, reported that John Paul had assured Beryl that Hart would have gotten out of the plane before the crash and had survived (Mark Charnley to the author, July 4, 2018, personal correspondence). John Paul's letter was prophetic for that is exactly how it happened. Bob Hart survived the crash and was a prisoner of war until the war's end.[26] The day after John Paul wrote that letter to Beryl, he boarded a Lupton's bomber and took off on his last mission.

25. "Incredible Story of the Dambusters Raid."
26. U.K. Allied Prisoners of War (1939–1945).

10

Final Mission

THE FATAL MISSION OF April 16, 1943 for Flying Officer Lupton's crew was a planned airstrike on Mannheim, Baden-Württemberg, Germany.[1] The city had been a target since 1940, and the bombing campaign had been relentless. On April 16, 1943, the silence of the night in Kirmington, England, was broken by the roar of twin-engine Wellington bombers lifting into the sky. Squadron 166 of British Bomber Command based in Kirmington had launched an attack on Mannheim, Germany, with a formation of twelve planes. They were to fly down the east coast of England to the English Channel, and after crossing the Channel, to their target: the industrial heartland of the German forces. The crew of John Paul's plane included Flying Officer Sidney Jacques Lupton (pilot), Flying Officer Roderick Alan Lord (navigator), Sergeant John Paul Merton (air observer/bomb aimer), Sergeant William Forster Whitfield (wireless operator), and Flying Officer Eric G. Hadingham (rear gunner). A pigeon in a cage was the last crew member to board the aircraft as the Royal Air Force used a homing pigeon as an unconventional emergency messaging system in the event of a plane crash: the pigeon, once released, returned to base with a message of the crash.[2] Plane crashes were common; the average life expectancy of the aver-

1. Unless otherwise noted, all information in this chapter is from John Paul Merton's RCAF service record: Ottawa, Canada, Library and Archives, "WWII Service Files of War Dead (1939–1947)."

2. "Use of Pigeons."

age crew member (average age of twenty-two years) was two weeks.[3] This was John Paul's seventh flight with the 166 Squadron.

The RCAF record shows that Lupton's Wellington aircraft took off Friday, April 16, 1943 at 21:19 hours. Throughout the war, Wellington twin engine medium longrange bombers lacked the fuel capacity for this long-distance flight. The Wellington had an air speed of 254 mph, a range of 1,540 miles, and a take-off weight of 29,500 pounds.[4] This mission was beyond its capacity, so the plane was outfitted with extra fuel tanks that were removed for shorter missions. Lupton was to fly from Kirmington, at an altitude of 13,000 feet, south along the east coast of England on this extra fuel. Once he reached Dungeness on the southeast coast of England, he was to switch from the extra fuel tanks to the regular fuel supply and proceed over the English Channel. Over the Channel, the pilot was instructed to descend gradually to an altitude of 1,500 feet by the time he reached the French coastline. The purpose for the low altitude was to pass through the German fighter aircraft belt over France. After crossing the French coastland, the pilot was to head to Germany and drop the payload over the target. When they reached near the target, they were to increase altitude in order to drop the bombs but avoid the blast. Lupton's Wellington bomber with a full load of 4,500 pounds of bombs never made it across the English Channel. Somewhere before reaching the coast of France, both engines cut out, and the plane began to rapidly lose altitude. At an altitude of 1,500 feet, Lupton's efforts to recover control or restart the engines were futile. With 4,500 pounds of bombs plus full fuel tanks, the plane went down fast. It crashed nose first at a ten-degree angle. The plane sank within seconds of hitting the water.

Hadingham's account from a letter to John Stanley (undated) tells the story in agonizing detail:

> The engines both cut and as we were carrying a full bomb and pet-
> rol load our descent from then on was very rapid. . . . I heard JPM
> (we knew him amongst the crew as Mert) ask for permission to
> open the bomb doors in order to jettison the bombs. F/O Lupton
> (the pilot) replied that it was too late and ordered us to prepare for
> immediate ditching. Seconds later we had crashed nose first into
> the sea. The sea was absolutely calm and it was bright moonlight.
> There was no noise apart from the aircraft continuing on their

3. "WW2: Could You Be Part."
4. "Vickers 417 Wellington Bomber."

> mission overhead. There was no one else to be seen and the dinghy took some time to appear on the surface in a partially inflated state. It was some distance away. . . . I made my way into it . . . not an easy feat when wearing bulky and sodden flying gear . . . F/O Allan Lord appeared and I was able to help him aboard. . . . Some time later (probably 3–4 minutes) we heard shouts for help. We paddled the dinghy over and came upon JPM. He was supporting Jack Lupton who appeared to be unconscious. It is difficult to determine time in these circumstances, but I would think he would have been supporting Jack Lupton for at least ten minutes, this whilst he was critically injured himself. An act of extreme bravery and selflessness which should have been recognized. . . . The pilot was unable to support himself and this meant that Allan Lord had to hold onto him whilst I attempted to help JPM aboard . . . JPM was unable to help and I found the task beyond me . . . by then we had presumed Jack Lupton to be dead he was released into the sea. . . . Allan Lord had to come to my assistance and together we managed to get him into the dinghy . . . it was obvious that JPM was very seriously injured . . . he was lucid for a period and was aware of his critical condition. *Most of the time he had left was spent in prayer* [italics added]. Shortly after the Bomb Aimer became delirious and about three hours later he died.

Lord, the navigator, wrote to Eric Hadingham from his hospital bed, telling him that he had recorded his memory of the event as soon afterward as he could:

> Mert was in the last stages of exhaustion being severely wounded about the forehead and unable to move from the waist down. I think probably his back was broken. In addition, he sank in the water until the sea had entered his mouth every time he shouted but it never occurred to him to let go of the pilot. He was an American, and if I ever hear another running down the Yankees in future, I shall have a word ready . . . . Eventually we had to let Lupton, the Pilot go, and after a great struggle we got the bombardier aboard. He was in great pain and soon became delirious, asking continuously for water, which we couldn't give him . . . . He died in the early morning.[5]

From the early hours (0400 hours) of Saturday, April 17, 1943 (the next day was Palm Sunday), the body of John Paul lay in the dinghy covered by a tarp. The wreck occurred in the English Channel, near the Somme

5. "Archive Report: Allied Forces."

estuary; the dinghy drifted in the channel, once coming dangerously near the coast of Calais, France, where it could have been discovered by German patrol boats. At one point, it was nearly swept into the North Sea. By the evening of Monday, April 19, 1943, Lord and Hadingham had given up hope of a quick rescue and could no longer keep John Paul's body in the dinghy. Lifting him overboard as best they could, and, as Hadingham described the event, "in as Christian manner" as possible, they let John Paul's body slip into the sea to join the bodies of Lupton, Whitfield, and multitudes of others who died in service to country and for freedom from tyranny. The remains of John Paul's body lie in repose on the floor of the English Channel. John Paul was twenty-four years old and had been married fifty-four days.

11

Aftermath

Lord and Hadingham

FIVE AND A HALF days after the crash, a British Hawker Typhoon on a re-connaissance mission broke away from its formation and circled Lord and Hadingham, who were still in the dinghy. When the plane spotted Lord and Hadingham, it waggled its wings in acknowledgment. The two downed airmen were rescued on Maundy Thursday before Easter 1943.[1]

There was an official enquiry into the crash by the Station Commander, which found no clear explanation of the cause: no pilot error was identified. The unofficial cause was assumed to be a mechanical failure (it may have been a faulty valve) during the switch-over from the extra fuel tanks to the main fuel supply line.[2]

Margaret May Merton

Margaret learned of the crash in a telegram, advising her that John Paul had died. According to John Paul's RCAF service record, on May 7, 1943, Flight Lieutenant Milton Foss of Bomber Command followed up his telegram and sent a letter, quoted below:[3]

1. See http://aircrewremembered.com/lupton-selwyn.html.

2. Ottawa, Canada, Library and Archives, "WWII Service Files of War Dead (1939–1947)."

3. Letters from Margaret May Merton to Bomber Command and the replies by

Dear Mrs. Merton,

It is with deep regret that I must confirm the information you have already received by telegram which stated that your husband lost his life as a result of air operations.

Your husband was an Air Bomber of a Wellington aircraft which took off to carry out bombing of Mannheim, Germany, on the night of the above-mentioned date. The aircraft encountered difficulties before reaching the target, however, and crashed into the sea causing severe wounds to your husband who died shortly after the crash.

Please accept my deepest sympathy with you in the loss of your husband.

Margaret lived with the news for a few days and had the support of her friends at Kedleston Hall. It was a bit much for her to wrap her mind and heart around at twenty-one years of age. She knew of others whose stories were similar but had turned out differently. There were reports of death when later it was learned that the person had survived. Indeed, that was the case with her friend Bob Hart.

On May 12, 1943, Margaret wrote to Bomber Command:

Dear Sir:

I had been living in hopes my husband was still alive and perhaps a prisoner of war. Would it be violating security if I asked you if some of the crew survived and had given you the information that my husband was severely injured or whether the Air Ministry had reports that the plane had been seen washing into the sea.

I am asking not because I cannot face the fact he may have been killed but because if there is any hope (after reading of so many men turning up after months) I shall go on hoping.

Thank you for your sympathy in my loss.

Yours sincerely,

Margaret M Merton

The reply came from Foss in a letter dated 18 May 1943:

Dear Mrs. Merton,

Thank you for your letter of May 12th, 1943, in which you request further information concerning your husband, Sergeant John Paul Merton.

There were two survivors of your husband's crew, Flying Officer R.S. Lord, Navigator, and Flying Officer E.G. Hadingham,

---

Bomber Command are in John Paul Merton's service file.

Rear Gunner, who reported that your husband was taken into the dinghy after the aircraft crashed but was in a serious condition and died soon afterwards and it was necessary to bury him at sea. I am attaching a copy of the statement by Flying Officer Lord.

May I again express my deepest sympathy with you in the loss of your husband.

Margaret's hopes were dashed. All that was left was her grief. She had endured the death of her mother when she was six years old. Now at twenty-one, she was a war widow. Her marriage of fifty-four days was over. She would have to reshape the life she had planned with John Paul.

Margaret May Merton was given John Paul's Operational Wings and a Certificate in recognition of his gallant service. This award was given after servicemen had flown ten operational sorties. She also received the Memorial Cross, an award given to the widow of servicemen who died in service to the country. His personal effects were given to her on August 24, 1943 and on October 10, 1943. The rosary he carried with him was in the package; it had not been with him when he prayed in the dinghy. His prayer books and the copy of Luke's gospel were among the effects returned to Margaret. [4]

The settlement of his estate took some time since he had drawn up a will as a single man in August 1942 in the United States and died a married man in England. After his death, Margaret had to wait for the legal issues to be settled in her favor. There was no acrimony and Margaret Merton and Rovene Miscall (executor of the estate) communicated directly with the attorneys to reach the outcome they knew John Paul would have wanted. [5]

Margaret told John Stanley in her letter of May 14, 1975 (private collection) that for the years immediately after John Paul's death, she spent her military leave time with John Paul's Aunt Gwynn Merton Trier and her husband Erwin, in West Horsley, Surrey. She commented that Gwynn's son Frank Merton Trier resembled John Paul in a startling way. Margaret also corresponded with Tom. When she remarried in 1946, Tom sent her a wedding gift of a copy of a book of his poems, *A Man in the Divided Sea*. Margaret noted in her May 14, 1975 letter to John Stanley that "I will never forget the spiritual comfort he [Tom] endeavored to give to me." Gertrude Merton, John Paul's paternal grandmother, sent Margaret a wedding cake when she remarried in 1946.

4. Ottawa, Canada, Library and Archives, "WWII Service Files of War Dead (1939–1947)."

5. Stanley, "Pigeon, Caged, Drowns," 14.

Tom Merton

On Holy Saturday, April 24, 1943, Tom found a letter from John Paul at his place at the table in the refectory and opened it the following Monday. At the time he did not know that John Paul had died. His reasons for waiting to read it for two days are not mentioned and suggest his priorities were elsewhere. John Paul described his wedding and honeymoon.

On Easter Monday, Tom wrote to John Paul. The letter was not mailed since the next day (April 27, 1943) Tom received a telegram from the Wing Commander of 166 Squadron dated April 17, 1943, informing him that his brother was reported missing in action. The telegram mentioned that he might be a prisoner of war. A few weeks later, Tom received the news that John Paul had died in the crash of his plane. [6]

Exactly when Tom wrote a twenty-eight-line poetic elegy expressing his grief at the death of his brother is not clear.[7] It begins by naming him "Sweet brother" and then lists the sacrifices Tom would endure if he could comfort his brother (overtones of Dante's Inferno seem intended). The remainder of the poem expresses concern for his soul. The poem has been analyzed by Patrick F. O'Connell, who notes that it is "more subtle, more dynamic, and more unified than a first impression might indicate."[8]

Michael Woodward, put the poem into the context of the relationship of the two brothers before offering a critique. Woodward wrote:

> That background [John Paul and Thomas's relationship] gives us an insight into the weight of emotion carried by the opening "Sweet brother." It has taken death to call this "sweet' forth. It contains Tom's remorse for past hostility, regret for the words never spoken, appreciation for what he has suddenly lost, the pathos of his brother's untimely death.[9]

The realization of the loss of his brother must have been profound and allowed his bond with John Paul to be expressed. Yet the poem still reflects Tom's image of his brother and not the actual person of his brother. Where the poem expresses concern for John Paul's soul he is referred to as "a poor

---

6. Merton, T., *Seven Storey Mountain*, 402.

7. Merton, T., *Seven Storey Mountain*, 404.

8. O'Connell, "Grief Transfigured," 10–15.

9. Woodward, "For My Brother," 70.

traveller" (line 6) whose "unhappy spirit lost its road" (line 10) and one who has a "weak and friendless hand" (line 24).[10]

One can only wonder how John Paul might have reacted reading this characterization of himself. The heartfelt emotion of brotherly affection that the poem captures had not been part of their relationship. While John Paul surely would have deeply valued the sentiment, he no doubt would not have recognized the description of his soul as a "poor traveller" who was unhappy or lost. The very positive, forward-thinking person that he was projects the image of a happily married man in the photo on his wedding day, and the few letters we have of his to friends during his time in England indicate that he was a man fighting a war with purpose and conviction. Nor was he friendless, neither in the recent nor remote past: Bob Hart named his son for John Paul, an indication of the endurance of the quality of his friendships (reported to the author by Mark Charnley, a friend of Bob Hart, in personal correspondence, July 4, 2018).

Tom's genuine and sincere expression of grief is clear. Once again there is an interpretation of John Paul that comes more from Tom's opinion than it does from an understanding of John Paul. Tom's opinions reflect his own manner of judging the actions of others at this time of his life. One can only wonder how the relationship of the two brothers might have changed as Tom grew into the depths of his eventual spiritual wisdom and had both been able to have the open and direct conversation John Paul had longed for his whole life.

10. Merton, T., *Seven Storey Mountain*, 404.

12

Inspiration

As reported by Lord and Hadingham, the plane crashed quickly, nose first, and hit the surface of the water at a ten-degree angle.[1] John Paul's position in the plane was in the nose of the Wellington, to the side of the pilot, where he lay prone on the floor, with his head forward, feet aft. He would have had the full force of the impact to his head and face upon impact. One can hardly imagine how he managed to escape from the plane (the nose would have been submerged by the impact), find and swim to Lupton in the dark, and hold Lupton in one arm while keeping both of them afloat using only one arm to tread water (Hadingham states that John Paul could not use his legs to assist with boarding the dinghy). The very fact that he was able to extricate himself from his position in the plane was miraculous: there was virtually no room in the bomber's position to turn around. John Paul was apparently paralyzed from the waist down. Hadingham noted "he [John Paul] was unable to help" when he and Lord tried to pull John Paul into the dinghy, and Lord notes that his back was likely broken. Unable to use his legs, John Paul was essentially a dead weight. Yet John Paul, wearing sodden flight gear and taking in a mouthful of seawater each time he yelled for help, kept himself and Lupton afloat for ten minutes by Hadingham's account. He swallowed water each time he shouted, indicating that he had tremendous difficulty staying afloat and was increasingly in jeopardy.

1. Unless otherwise noted, all information about the plane crash is from John Paul Merton's RCAF service record: Ottawa, Canada, Library and Archives, "WWII Service Files of War Dead (1939–1947)."

Hadingham himself had difficulty boarding the dinghy due to his wet fly-ing gear—it was "not an easy feat when wearing bulky and sodden flying gear"—yet John Paul supported the weight of himself and Lupton while enduring a bleeding head wound and other injuries and wearing that same "sodden" gear. John Paul held on to Lupton, refusing to believe he was dead, committed to saving him at all costs.

If John Paul had the use of his legs on impact and only lost their use as a result of damage caused by his efforts to save Lupton, that would mean he received further injury due to his life-saving efforts. Otherwise, we as-sume that John Paul was seriously wounded on impact such that first-hand accounts report him as paralyzed from the waist down. By either scenario, he sacrificed his own life for the sake of another. Hadingham, in his cor-respondence with John Stanley, considered it an act of bravery and selfless-ness that ought to have been recognized.

At the end of his life, John Paul's faith sustained and comforted him. In the dinghy, covered by the tarp, he prayed. Grace from his recent bap-tism and his lifelong quest for belonging led him to turn in this hour to God, his true father whom he had sought all his life. He had lived his law of love to its fullest sense. His response to the pilot's plight was immediate and without hesitation: he gave his life to try to save Lupton because that was his nature, his very essence.

The energy released in John Paul in order for him to rescue Lupton was more than the energy of his psychological makeup as a humble, opti-mistic, and caring person. It was more than the energy one gets from be-ing a comrade-in-arms; it was certainly more than the energy one gets by throwing caution to the winds. The source of his energy came from the deepest part of his soul—who God created him to be.

John Paul's spiritual energy had been a driving force all his life. He knew himself, and in that moment when he found the pilot in distress, he acted from the center of his being—not from any external motive but from his identity in God. He had reached out for much of his life to care for the "other," and in this moment, acted from his authentic true self.

Some may think he was a hero. John Paul would say he was simply do-ing what he must do, what was natural: it took no effort and it was easy. He did not consider the desires of others or the accepted or prescribed means of behavior: he took the action that was right for him. He acted in a manner true to his identity as God created him.

John Paul acted without regard for the danger, without thought, but with spontaneity. Athletes and performers speak of being "in the flow" or "in the zone." Acting from this place requires no thought: it is immediate and can result in extraordinary performance. His decision was easy, but not without consequences. John Paul hit the water headfirst and sustained major injuries, yet when he discovered Lupton, he did not think about what to do. Somehow, paralyzed from the waist down, he swam to save him.

Having sacrificed his body, without water to quench his thirst, John Paul spent his last three hours in communion with God, praying aloud until his death. Tom compared this event to the three hours of the thirst of Jesus during the crucifixion.[2] On the evening of April 19, 1943, Hadingham and Lord consigned John Paul's body to the depths of the English Channel, "in as Christian manner as possible." He was consigned, not to a tomb, but to the care of God, in a final emptying of self, like a Carthusian monk who is buried anonymously in a space marked by a wooden cross with no name inscribed upon it. Finally, he was home, his soul united to the one true Father.

Of John Paul's law of love, lived out from the time he was five years old, Tom wrote:

> But now that Christ has laid down His life and risen from the dead, to take possession of us by His Spirit, the Spirit himself, dwelling in us, should be to us a law. This interior law, the "New Law" which is purely a *law of love* [italics added] infuses the soul so that doing the will of God is done, not with fear, but with spontaneous love.[3]

To the casual observer, John Paul Merton's life was marked by tragedy and failure: born to parents who were starving artists—a mother who died when he was still a baby, a father who never chose to parent his children— he was unable to complete a college degree or to achieve his pilot's wings. His marriage lasted only 54 days, ending in his death. Yet a closer look reveals a man whose life touched many others, a man with a great, open, and loving heart who apparently never knew an enemy and saw in others only the potential for friendship. People liked him immediately because John Paul radiated a deep reverence for every human being. At the end of his life, in one shining moment, he sacrificed himself to give another man a chance to return to his family. There is no greater love.

2. Merton, T., *Seven Storey Mountain*, 403.

3. Merton, T., *Life and Holiness*, 37.

13

Memorials

Military

MEMORIALS IN PUBLIC SQUARES, military museums, and political assemblies are places where people can pause for a moment and remember the sacrifices made by many for the sake of the rest. Following his death, John Paul Merton was no longer unknown or forgotten. Military tributes, as well as personal praise, were forthcoming. The manner of his service, his character, and his heroism were recognized and honored.

- John Paul Merton is one of the 379 Americans who are remembered with their names inscribed on the Memorial Wall of the Bomber Command Museum in Ottawa, Canada.[1]

- John Paul Merton's name is inscribed on page 194 in the Books of Remembrance that lie in the Memorial Chamber of the Peace Tower on Parliament Hill, Ottawa, Canada.[2]

- John Paul Merton's name is inscribed in Panel 186 on the Royal Air Force Memorial to the Missing (a memorial for those with no known grave) at Runneymede Memorial, Surrey, United Kingdom.[3]

- The president of Cornell University sent a letter of condolence to Harold Jenkins and his family with the news that John Paul's name would

1. "379 Americans."
2. "Sergeant John Paul Merton."
3. "John Paul Merton."

be added to the Roll of Honor of Cornellians who had died in the war. The university commissioned the stained-glass window of the Cornell World War II Memorial in Anabel Taylor Hall, where John Paul Merton is memorialized.[4]

- The city of Ithaca, New York, built a WWII Memorial in the center of town, which includes the name John Paul Merton.

Personal

Of all these war memorials, the most significant are from his fellow crew members, those who knew him best. The two men who survived the crash of the fateful Wellington bomber, Lord and Hadingham, who observed John Paul's heroism, were forthcoming in their honor of John Paul. Lord wrote, "He was an American, and if I ever hear another running down of Yankees in future, I shall have a word ready."[5]

Mark Charnley, a friend of Bob Hart, who was John Paul's closest friend, reported to the author (Charnley email to the author, July 4, 2018) that Hart spoke often of John Paul, telling his story to all who were interested. Hart named his son after John Paul: Jonathan Paul Wesley Hart.

4. Cornell University Veterans Memorials, "Annabel Taylor Hall."
5. See http://aircrewremembered.com/lupton-selwyn.html.

14

The Rest of the Story

The following lists the outcome of events for people who knew John Paul and were part of his life, and for places significant to his story.

- Flight Officers Lord and Hadingham were rescued following five days adrift in the English Channel. Both men returned to duty; both survived the war.

- Royal Air Force Kirmington Airfield was placed on Care and Maintenance status in December 1945 and closed in 1953. After years of disuse, it was refurbished and renamed "Humberside International Airport" in the 1970s. The "scramble bell" of the 166 Squadron hangs at the entrance. The villagers continue to remember the men of the 166 Squadron with an annual memorial service.[1]

- Margaret May Merton remained in the Auxiliary Territorial Service until the end of the war. She married Norman John Kirkman in the summer of 1946.[2] She lived in Birkenhead, Merseyside, until her death on April 7, 1992.

- Tom, who adopted the professed religious name of Father Louis Merton, O.C.S.O. wrote more than sixty books on spirituality, peace and justice, and ecumenism. He died from accidental electrocution on December 10, 1968 while attending a conference on monasticism

---

1. "Kirmington Airfield History."
2. England and Wales, Civil Registration Marriage Index (1916–2005).

in Bangkok, Thailand.[3] His funeral Mass and burial service were held on December 17, 1968 at the Trappist Abbey of Gethsemani in what is now known as Trappist, Kentucky. He was buried in the monastic cemetery.

- Harold Jenkins died in Flushing, Queens, New York, in 1972, and his wife, Elsie, died in 1990.[4]

- Robert Wesley Hart married Beryl Yvonne Jones in West Ham, Essex, England in 1945.[5] Their son, Jonathan Paul Wesley Hart, was born February 26, 1950 in Bromley, England and was named after John Paul Merton.[6]

- Robert Hart died in 1996, and his wife Beryl died in 2001.[7]

- Len Miscall rose to the rank of captain in the U.S. Navy and worked on the rebuilding of Pearl Harbor.[8] He died on August 2, 1980.[9]

- Rovene Miscall died March 5, 1991.[10]

- Marilynn Miscall was a ceramic artist in Ithaca, New York. She married Sydney Eighmey.[11] She died in 1999.

Below is a timeline of the major events of John Paul's short life.

Table 3—Major Events in the Life of John Paul Merton

DATE	AGE	EVENT
Nov 2, 1918		Birth, Douglaston, Queens County, New York, NY
Oct 3, 1921	2	Death of mother, New York, New York
June 1929	10	Baptism, Zion Episcopal Church, Douglaston, NY
April 1930	11	Confirmation, Cathedral of St. John the Divine, New York, NY
January 18, 1931	12	Death of father, London, England

3. Reports of Deaths of American Citizens Abroad.
4. U.S. Social Security Death Index (1935–2014).
5. England and Wales, Civil Registration Marriage Index (1916–2005).
6. England and Wales, Civil Registration Birth Index (1916–2007).
7. England and Wales, Civil Registration Death Index (1916–2007).
8. U.S. Navy Support Books (1901–1902, 1917–2010).
9. U.S. Social Security Death Index (1935–2014).
10. U.S. Social Security Death Index (1935–2014).
11. New York State, Marriage Index (1881–1967).
U.S. Social Security Death Index (1935–2014).

May 1935	16	Graduation, Gettysburg Academy, Gettysburg, PA
September 1935	16	Freshman, Cornell University, Ithaca, NY
October 1936	17	Death of maternal grandfather, Sam Jenkins
August 1937	18	Death of maternal grandmother Martha Jenkins
June 1940	21	Permanent dismissal from Cornell
August 25, 1941	22	Enlists, Royal Canadian Air Force
May 23, 1942	23	Receives Air Observer brevet, promoted to Sergeant
July 1942	23	Visits brother Tom, Gethsemani monastery, Bardstown, KY
July 26, 1942	23	Catholic Baptism, St. Catherine Church, New Haven, KY
February 23, 1943	24	Marriage to Margaret May Evans, Birkenhead, UK
April 17, 1943	24	Death after crash of RAF Wellington bomber in English Channel
April 20, 1943	24	Body consigned to burial at sea

Epilogue

Relying on available records and the comments of those who knew him, I have tried to bring to light the person of John Paul Merton. The records speak for themselves. The comments about him made by his family, high school faculty, friends of his brother, Royal Canadian Air Force instructors, war time mates, and his wife reveal a person who was neither saint nor scholar but kind and liked by all. His wife captured his essence with the remark that he was a gentle man who loved his faith.

What I hope has been made clear in this book is that he did not accomplish this of his own doing. Grace perfects nature (the self) and grace was manifested in the way he dealt with the people and events of his life, though he may not have been aware that he was being guided on his path. He lived his law of love from his earliest days until his final day. John Paul Merton lived an ordinary life and was an extraordinary person by simply being who he was. In doing so he lights the path for each of us to follow.

Bibliography

"The 379 Americans." Bomber Command Museum of Canada. https://www.bombercommandmuseum.ca/bomber-command/the-379-americans/.

"Anabel Taylor Hall." Cornell University Veterans Memorials. https://veteransmemorials.cornell.edu/anabel-taylor-hall/.

"Archive Report: Allied Forces." http://aircrewremembered.com/lupton-selwyn.html

Barrow, Mandy. "Food Rationing." http://www.primaryhomeworkhelp.co.uk/war/rationing.htm.

"Black Tom 1916 Bombing." Federal Bureau of Investigation (FBI) History. https://www.fbi.gov/history/famous-cases/black-tom-1916-bombing.

"The Blitz." Encyclopedia Britannica. https://www.britannica.com/event/the-Blitz.

"The Blitz: The Hardest Night 10/11 May 1941, 11:02pm–05:57am." Royal Air Force Museum. https://www.rafmuseum.org.uk/research/online-exhibitions/history-of-the-battle-of-britain/the-blitz-the-hardest-night/.

The Bradford Annual Catalog (1908–1909). Bradford Alumni Association. The Special Collections Division of Haverhill Library, Haverhill, MA.

Caine, Phillip D. *Eagles of the RAF: The World War II Eagle Squadrons*. Washington, DC: National Defense University Press, 1991.

"Campus History and Description." Bradford Alumni Association. http://www.bradfordalumni.org/bradfordcampushistory/history.html.

"Canadian Virtual War Memorial." Veterans Affairs Canada. https://www.veterans.gc.ca/eng/remembrance/memorials/canadian-virtual-war-memorial/.

Cardiganshire, Wales. Anglican Baptisms, Marriages, and Burials (1633–1993). https://www.ancestry.com.

Chess, Stella, and Alexander Thomas. *Temperament in Clinical Practice*. New York: Guilford, 1986.

"Clan Grierson History." ScotClans. https://www.scotclans.com/scottish-clans/clan-grierson/grierson-history.

Collins, Roger. "A Sense of Construction: The Life and Work of Owen Merton." Unpublished manuscript, last modified in 2006.

"CPI Inflation Calculator." U.S. Bureau of Labor Statistics. https://www.bls.gov /data/inflation_calculator.htm.

Daggy, Robert E. "Birthday Theology: A Reflection on Thomas Merton and the Bermuda Menage." *The Kentucky Review* 7 (1987) 61–89.

———. "A Great Soul: Owen Merton." *The Merton Seasonal* 11 (1986) 2–4.

"Do Catholic Parents Have to Raise Their Children as Catholic?" Canon Law Made Easy. https://canonlawmadeeasy.com/2009/01/22/do-catholic-parents-have-to-raise-their-children-as-catholics/.

"The Eagle Squadrons of WWII: American Volunteers Fly with the Royal Air Force." American Battle Monuments Commission. https://www.abmc.gov/news-events/news/eagle-squadrons-wwii-american-volunteers-fly-royal-air-force.

England and Wales, Civil Registration Birth Index (1916–2007). https://www.ancestry.com.

England and Wales, Civil Registration Death Index (1916–2007). https://www.ancestry.com.

England and Wales, Civil Registration Marriage Index (1916–2005). General Register Office, United Kingdom, Marriage Register Indexes. https://www.ancestry.com.

England Census Class RG14, Place 6873 (1911). Piece 6873, Schedule Number 100. https://www.ancestry.com.

England, Select Marriages, (1538–1973). https://www.ancestry.com.

Forest, James. *Living with Wisdom: A Life of Thomas Merton*. Rev. ed. New York: Orbis, 2008.

———. *Thomas Merton: A Pictorial Biography*. New York: Harcourt Brace, 1948.

Fox, James. "The Spiritual Son." In *Thomas Merton, Monk: A Monastic Tribute*, edited by Patrick Hart, 141–60. New York: Sheed and Ward, 1974.

Furlong, Monica. *Merton: A Biography*. Toronto: Bantam, 1981.

"Germans Unleash U-Boats." History.com. https://www.history.com/this-day-in-history/germans-unleash-u-boats.

Giroux, Robert. "Introduction." In *The Seven Storey Mountain,* by Thomas Merton, xi–xviii. 50th Anniversary edition. New York: Harcourt, 1998.

Hadingham, Eric G. to John Stanley, undated correspondence. Paper. Private collection.

Halliday, Hugh A. "Canada's Yanks: Air Force, Part 16." *Legion Magazine*, Jul 1, 2006. https://legionmagazine.com/en/2006/07/canadas-yanks/.

Hempstead-Milton, S. "Merton's Search for Paradise and His Integration of Ruth Merton, Sophia, and Mary." *The Merton Seasonal* 21 (1996) 9–14.

———. "Shared Facts, Different Stories: The Mother of Thomas Merton." *The Merton Journal* 7 (2000) 36–50.

"History." Zion Episcopal Church. https://zionepiscopal.org/about-us/history/

"Kedleston Hall." Heritage Emergencies and Great Estates. http://www.heritageemergency.org/kedleston-hall/.

"Huber Hall." Gettysburg College. Transformative Places, Resilient Spaces. https://www.gettysburg.edu/news/stories?id=dee02b07-33e7-4ce6-985e-eed77423d127.

"The Incredible Story of the Dambusters Raid." Imperial War Museums. https://www.iwm.org.uk/search/global?query=ruhr&pageSize=.

"Inflation Calculator." Bank of England. https://www.bankofengland.co.uk/monetary-policy/inflation/inflation-calculator.

Jenkins, Ruth to Percyval Tudor-Hart, 20 December 1911. In "Sense of Construction: The Life and Work of Owen Merton," by Roger Collins, unpublished manuscript.

——— to Percyval Tudor-Hart, 23 August 1912 in "Sense of Construction: The Life and Work of Owen Merton," by Roger Collins, unpublished manuscript.

"John Paul Merton." Commonwealth War Graves Commission, Runnymede Memorial. https://www.cwgc.org/find-records/find-war-dead/casualty-details/1076758/john-paul-merton/.

Kirkman, Margaret Evans Merton to John Stanley, May 14, 1975. Private collection. Paper file.

"Kirmington Airfield History." Bomber County Aviation Resource. https://www.bcar.org. uk/kirmington-history.

"Kneel." Episcopal Dictionary of the Church. https://www.episcopalchurch.org/glossary/ kneel/.

"Wadleigh High School for Girls/(now) Wadleigh High School." Landmarks Preservation Commission of New York City. http://s-media.nyc.gov/agencies/lpc/lp/1840.pdf.

"Last Graduation Held by Academy Friday Morning." *Gettysburg Compiler*, Jun 15, 1935. https://news.google.com/newspapers?id=8SczAAAAIBAJ&dq=round-top%20 tower&pg=6424%2C298910.

"The Liverpool Blitz." Imperial War Museums. https://www.iwm.org.uk/history/the-liverpool-blitz.

London, England, Church of England Marriages and Banns (1754–1932). London Metropolitan Archives; London, England; Reference Number dro/116/a/02/002 100. https://www.ancestry.com.

Meade, Mark. "Thomas Merton's Censored Struggle with Suicide." *The Merton Journal* 23 (2016) 3–15.

Meegan, William J. "The Maternal Ancestors of Thomas Merton." *The Merton Seasonal* 47.3 (Fall 2022): 3-12.

————. "Paternal Ancestors of Thomas Merton: 1652–1968." *The Merton Seasonal* 46 (2021) 15–22.

Mehuron, Tamar A. "The Eagle Squadrons." *Air & Space Forces Magazine*, Oct 1, 2007. https://www.airforcemag.com/article/1007eagle/.

"Merton, John Paul." Canada's Bomber Command Virtual Memorial. https://www. bombercommandmuseum.ca/memorial/.

Merton, John Paul. Cornell Transcript (1935–1940). Registrar, Cornell University.

Merton, John Paul to Tom O'Brien, February 2, 1942. Paper. Archives of the Thomas Merton Center at Bellarmine University, Louisville, Kentucky.

————. to Tom O'Brien, undated. Paper. Archives of the Thomas Merton Center at Bellarmine University, Louisville, Kentucky.

Merton, Owen to Percyval Tudor-Hart, January 22, 1921. "'An Owen Merton Letter,' edited and introduced by Robert E. Daggy." *The Merton Seasonal* 11 (1986) 10–11.

Merton, Ruth. "Come into the Kitchen." *American Cookery* 26 (1922) 606–8.

————. "The Tiny House." *American Cookery* 26 (1921) 182–85.

————. *Tom's Book: To Granny with Tom's Best Love, 1916.* Edited by Sheila Milton. Monterey: Larkspur, 2001.

Merton, Thomas. *Life and Holiness.* New York: Herder & Herder, 1963.

————. *The Road to Joy: Letters to New and Old Friends.* Edited by Robert Daggy. New York: Farrar, Straus & Giroux, 1989.

————. *Run to the Mountain: The Story of a Vocation (1939–1941).* Vol. 1 of *The Journals of Thomas Merton,* edited by Patrick Hart. San Francisco: HarperCollins, 1995.

————. *The Seven Storey Mountain.* 50th Anniversary edition. New York: Harcourt, 1998.

————. *The Sign of Jonas.* New York: Harcourt Brace, 1953.

————. *Turning Toward the World (The Pivotal Years, 1960–1963).* Vol. 4 of *The Journals of Thomas Merton,* edited by Victor A. Kramer. San Francisco: HarperCollins, 1996.

Milton, Sheila M. "Introduction to 'The Tiny House' by Ruth Merton." *The Merton Seasonal* 21 (2004) 9–17.

"Mission and Vision." Wadleigh School. https://www.wadleighharts.org.

Mott, Michael. *The Seven Mountains of Thomas Merton.* Boston: Houghton Mifflin, 1984.

"Neutrality Acts, 1930s." U.S. State Department, Office of the Historian. https://history. state.gov/milestones/1921–1936/neutrality-acts.

New York. "Abstracts of WWI Military Service (1917–1919)."

New York City Health Department. Death Certificates: Certificate 22879. https://www1. nyc.gov/site/doh/services/death-certificates.page.

New York, Extracted Death Index (1862–1948). New York City Department of Records/ Municipal Archives. https://www.ancestry.com.

New York, Marriage License Indexes (1907–2018). New York City Municipal Archives, New York, New York. Borough: Manhattan, Volume 7. https://www.ancestry.com.

New York, New York, Birth Index (1910–1965). https://www.ancestry.com.

New York, New York, U.S. Index to Death Certificates (1862–1948). New York City Department of Records and Information Services, New York City Death Certificates, Borough of Queens (1937). https://www.ancestry.com.

New York, Passenger Lists (1820–1957). 1910 Arrival in New York, New York. Microfilm Serial T715 (1897–1957). Microfilm Roll 1569, Line 20, Page 154. https://www. ancestry.com.

New York, Passenger Lists (1820–1957). 1922 Arrival in New York, New York. Microfilm Serial T715 (1897–1957). Microfilm Roll 3089, Line 12, Page 48. https://www. ancestry.com.

New York, Passenger Lists (1897–1957). 1923 Arrival in New York, New York. Microfilm Serial T715, Microfilm Roll 2373, Line 6, Page 97. https://www.ancestry.com.

New York, Passenger and Crew Lists (including Castle Garden and Ellis Island) (1820– 1957). 1916 Arrival in New York, New York. Microfilm Serial T715 (1897–1957). Microfilm Roll 2484, Line 17, Page 32. https://www.ancestry.com.

New York, Passenger and Crew Lists (including Castle Garden and Ellis Island) (1820– 1957). 1925 Arrival in New York, New York. Microfilm Serial: T715 (1897–1957). Microfilm Roll 3676, Line 10, Page 134. https://www.ancestry.com.

New York, Passenger and Crew Lists (including Castle Garden and Ellis Island) (1820– 1957). 1926 Arrival in New York, New York. Microfilm Serial: T715 (1897–1957). Microfilm Roll 3912, Line: 9, Page 98. https://www.ancestry.com.

New York, Passenger and Crew Lists (including Castle Garden and Ellis Island) (1820– 1957. 1930 Arrival in New York, New York. Microfilm Serial: T715 (1897–1957). Microfilm Roll 4797, Line 20, Page 15. https://www.ancestry.com.

New York, Passenger and Crew Lists (including Castle Garden and Ellis Island), (1820– 1957). 1930 Arrival in New York, New York. Microfilm Serial: T715 (1897–1957). Microfilm Roll 482, Line 18; Page 195. https://www.ancestry.com.

New York, Passenger and Crew Lists (including Castle Garden and Ellis Island), (1820– 1957). 1931 Arrival in New York, New York. Microfilm Serial: T715 (1897–1957). Microfilm Roll 5012, Line 2, Page 216. https://www.ancestry.com.

New York, Passenger Lists (1820–1957). 1932 Arrival in New York, New York. Microfilm Serial T715 (1897–1957). Microfilm Roll 5216, Line 10, Page 26. https://www. ancestry.com.

New York, Passenger and Crew Lists (including Castle Garden and Ellis Island) (1820– 1957). 1933 Arrival in New York, New York. Microfilm Serial T715 (1897–1957). Microfilm Roll 5311, Line 2, Page 83. https://www.ancestry.com.

New York, Passenger and Crew Lists (including Castle Garden and Ellis Island) (1820–1957). 1934 Arrival in New York, New York. Microfilm Serial T715 (1897–1957). Microfilm Roll 5504, Line 8, Page 122. https://www.ancestry.com.

New York State Census (1925). New York State Archives, Albany, New York. State Population Census Schedules (1925). Election District 14, Assembly District 02, City: North Hempstead, County: Nassau, 20. https://www.ancestry.com.

New York State Census (1925). New York State Archives, Albany, New York. State Population Census Schedules (1925). Election District 56, Assembly District 04. City: New York, County: Queens. Page 76A. https://www.ancestry.com.

New York State Marriage Index (1881–1967). https://www.ancestry.com.

New Zealand, Birth Index (1840–1950). https://www.ancestry.com.

New Zealand, Registers of Medical Practitioners and Nurses (1882–1933). https://www.ancestry.com.

New Zealand, School Registers and Lists (1850–1967). https://www.ancestry.com.

New Zealand, Teacher and Civil Service Examinations and Licenses (1880–1920). https://www.ancestry.com.

"Obituary: Samuel Jenkins." *The Publisher's Weekly*, Nov 7, 1936.

"Obituary: Owen Merton." *The Press*, 67, no. 20176, Mar 3, 1931. https://paperspast.natlib.govt.nz/newspapers/CHP19310303.2117.

O'Connell, Patrick. "Grief Transfigured: Merton's Elegy on His Brother." *The Merton Seasonal* 18 (1993) 10–15.

Ohio, Births and Christenings Index (1774–1973). https://www.ancestry.com.

Ohio, County Marriage Records (1774–1993). https://www.ancestry.com.

Ottawa, Canada, Library and Archives. "WWII Service Files of War Dead (1939–1947)." Series RG 24, Volume 28233.

"Owen Heathcote Grierson Merton." Find a Grave. https://www.findagrave.com/memorial/177237740/owen-heathcote_grierson-merton

"Personal Items." *The Press*, Feb 22, 1911. https://www.ancestry.com.

"PS 98 School History." PS 98Q-The Douglaston School. https://www.ps98q.org/school-history.

"RCAF Sequence of Training Chart." Commonwealth Air Training Plane Museum and RCAF WWII Memorial. https://airmuseum.ca/about/the-bcatp/rcaf-sequence-of-training-chart/.

Reports of Deaths of American Citizens Abroad. https://www.ancestry.com.

Research Information of the Auxiliary Territorial Service (ATS). "Auxiliary Territorial Service." Forces of War Records. https://www.forces-war-records.co.uk/units/131/auxiliary-territorial-service.

Rice, Edward. "Accuracy in Merton: A Plan for Getting the Facts Right." *The Merton Seasonal*, 11 (1986) 14–15.

———. *The Man in the Sycamore Tree: The Good Times and Hard Life of Thomas Merton: An Entertainment with Photographs*. San Diego: Harcourt Brace Jovanovich, 1985.

"Ruth Calvert Jenkins Merton." Find a Grave. https://www.findagrave.com/memorial/5054974/ruth-calvert-merton.

"Sergeant John Paul Merton." The Canadian Virtual War Memorial/Government of Canada. https://www.veterans.gc.ca/eng/remembrance/memorials/canadian-virtual-war-memorial/detail/1076758?John%20Paul%20Merton.

Shannon, William. "Note to the Reader." In *The Seven Storey Mountain*, by Thomas Merton, xix xxiii. 50th Anniversary edition. New York: Harcourt, 1998.

"Spanish Flu." https://www.history.com/topics/world-war-i/1918-flu-pandemic.

Stanley, John. "The Pigeon, Caged, Drowns." Unpublished manuscript, last modified in 1987. Division of Rare and Manuscript Collections, Cornell University Library, John Stanley, Writings #4307. Adobe Acrobat file.

Thomas, Alexander, et al. "New York Longitudinal Study, 1956–1988." Harvard Dataverse V2, 1998. https://doi.org/10.7910/DVN/CIGGJY.2.

Trail, Richard R. "Thomas Izod Bennett." Royal College of Physicians. https://history.rcplondon.ac.uk/inspiring-physicians/thomas-izod-bennett.

U.K. Allied Prisoners of War (1939–1945). The National Archives, Kew, London, England; WO 392 POW Lists (1943–1945). Reference Number: WO 392/21. https://www.ancestry.com.

U.K. Incoming Passenger Lists (1878–1960). The National Archives of the U.K., Kew, Surrey, England. Board of Trade: Commercial and Statistical Department and successors, Inwards Passenger Lists, Class BT26, Piece 439. https://www.ancestry.com.

U.K. Incoming Passenger Lists (1878–1960). The National Archives of the U.K., Kew, Surrey, England. Board of Trade: Commercial and Statistical Department and successors, Inwards Passenger Lists, Class BT26, Piece 598. https://www.ancestry.com.

U.K. Incoming Passenger Lists (1878–1960). The National Archives of the U.K., Kew, Surrey, England. Board of Trade: Commercial and Statistical Department and successors, Inwards Passenger Lists, Class: BT26; Piece 804. https://www.ancestry.com.

U.K. Incoming Passenger Lists (1878–1960). The National Archives of the U.K., Kew, Surrey, England. Board of Trade: Commercial and Statistical Department and successors, Inwards Passenger Lists, Class BT26, Piece 828. https://www.ancestry.com.

U.K. Incoming Passenger Lists (1878–1960). The National Archives of the U.K., Kew, Surrey, England. Board of Trade: Commercial and Statistical Department and successors. Inwards Passenger Lists, Class: BT26, Piece 875. https://www.ancestry.com.

U.K. Incoming Passenger Lists (1878–1960). The National Archives of the U.K., Kew, Surrey, England. Board of Trade: Commercial and Statistical Department and successors. Inwards Passenger Lists, Class BT26, Piece 935. https://www.ancestry.com.

U.K. Outward Passenger Lists (1890-1960). The National Archives of the U.K., Kew, Surrey, England. Board of Trade: Commercial and Statistical Department and successors. https://www.ancestry.com.

U.S. City Directories, New York, NY (1822–1995). https://www.ancestry.com.

U.S. City Directories, Zanesville, OH (1822–1995). https://www.ancestry.com.

U.S. Federal Census (1870). Zanesville, Muskingum County, Ohio, Ward 14. Roll M593_1251, 526B. Family History Library Film 552750. https://www.ancestry.com.

U.S. Federal Census (1880). Zanesville, Muskingum County, Ohio. Roll 1054, 375B, Enumeration District 177. https://www.ancestry.com.

U.S. Federal Census (1920). Brooklyn Assembly District 7, Kings County, New York. Roll T625_115, Page 2A, Enumeration District 388. https://www.ancestry.com.

U.S. Federal Census (1920). Queens Assembly District 4, Queens County, New York. Roll T625_1233, Page 4B. Enumeration District 216. https://www.ancestry.com.

U.S. Federal Census (1930). Manhattan, New York. FHL microfilm 2341295, Page 1B, Enumeration District 0502. https://www.ancestry.com.

U.S. Federal Census (1930). Queens, New York. Enumeration District 0957. https://www.ancestry.com.

U.S. Federal Census (1940). Ithaca, Thompkins County, New York. Roll M-T0627–02793, Page 2A. Enumeration District 55–30. https://www.ancestry.com.

U.S. Navy Support Books (1901–1902, 1917–2010). https://www.ancestry.com.

U.S. Passport Applications (1795–1925). https://www.ancestry.com.

U.S. Quaker Meeting Records (1681–1935). Guilford College; Greensboro, North Carolina; Women's Minutes (1779–1843). Collection: North Carolina Yearly Meeting Minutes. https://www.ancestry.com.

U.S. School Yearbooks (1880–2012). *The Columbian* (1911). https://www.ancestry.com.

U.S. School Yearbooks (1900–1990). *The Cornellian* (1936). https://www.ancestry.com.

U.S. School Yearbooks (1900–1990). *OSOGA Yearbook* (1934). https://www.ancestry.com.

U.S. Social Security Death Index (1935–2014). https://www.ancestry.com.

U.S. World War I Draft Registration Cards (1917–1918). New York, Registration County: Kings, Roll 1754308, Draft Board 41. https://www.ancestry.com.

U.S. World War I Draft Registration Cards (1917–1918). New York, Registration County: Queens, Roll 1818488, Draft Board 185. https://www.ancestry.com.

U.S. World War II Draft Registration Cards (1926–1975). The National Archives at St. Louis, MO. Fourth Registration for the State of Maryland. Records of the Selective Service System, (1926–1975). Record Group Number 147, Series Number M1939. https://www.ancestry.com.

"The Use of Pigeons by the RAF in WW2." ARCRE. https://www.arcre.com/pigeons/pigeonsraf.

"Vickers 417 Wellington Bomber." Flugzeug Info Net. http://www.flugzeuginfo.net/acdata_php/acdata_wellington_en.php.

Wallis, Barnes. "Geodetics." http://sirbarneswallis.com/Geodetics.htm.

"Women in Uniform." U.K. National Archives. http://www.nationalarchives.gov.uk/womeninuniform/wwii_intro.htm.

Woodward, Michael. "For My Brother: Reported Missing in Action, 1943." *Oakham Papers* (2000) 69–74. https://thomasmertonsociety.org/Dark/Woodward.pdf.

"Worldwide Deaths in World War II." National WWII Museum. https://www.nationalww2museum.org/students-teachers/student-resources/research-starters/research-starters-worldwide-deaths-world-war.

Worthington, Everett L. *Forgiveness and Reconciliation: Theory and Practice.* New York: Routledge, Taylor & Francis, 2014.

"WW2: Could You Be Part of a Lancaster Bomber Crew?" https://www.bbc.co.uk/teach/ww2-could%20-you-be-part-of-a-lancaster-bomber-crew/zd2v6v4.